Scotland Church of

The National Covenant and Solemn League and Covenant

With the acknowledgement of sins, and engagement to duties as they

were renewed at Lesmahego, March 3. 1688 with accommodation to the

present times

.

Scotland Church of

The National Covenant and Solemn League and Covenant
With the acknowledgement of sins, and engagement to duties as they were
renewed at Lesmahego, March 3. 1688 with accommodation to the present times

ISBN/EAN: 9783337248543

Printed in Europe, USA, Canada, Australia, Japan

Cover: Foto ©Suzi / pixelio.de

More available books at **www.hansebooks.com**

THE
NATIONAL COVENANT

AND

SOLEMN·LEAGUE & COVENANT;

With the

ACKNOWLEDGEMENT of SINS,

AND

ENGAGEMENT to DUTIES:

As they were Renewed at *Lesmahego, March* 3. with Accommodation to the Present Times.

TOGETHER WITH

An *Introduction* touching *National Covenants*, by way of *Analysis* on the 29th. Chapter of *Deuteronomy*. The Substance whereof, was delivered in a Discourse to the People, on the *Preparation day*, before they were Renewed.

Isaiah 24. 5. *The Earth is also defiled under the Inhabitants thereof ; because they have transgressed the Laws, changed the Ordinance, broken the Everlasting Covenant.*
Ezekiel 17. 18. *Seing he despised the Oath, by breaking the Covenant, when lo, he had given his hand, and hath done all these things, he shall not escape.*

Printed in the 40th. Year of Our Publick Breach of Covenant : The Year wherein there was much Zeal for *Confderating* among *Men*, but little for *Covenanting* with GOD.

An *Introduction*, touching **National Covenants**, by way of *Analysis*, on the *29th* Chapter of *Deuteronomy*. The substance whereof, was delivered in a Discourse to the People, on the *Preparation-Day* before the Renewing of the **Covenants** at *Lesmahego*.

THE greatest Glory of Man, and the lowest, and yet the most loving and lovely step of *G O D S Condescension* towards Man, was, is, and shall be, that he is admitted into a Covenant Relation with GOD, whereby the Lord becomes his GOD, King, Master, Husband, Father; And he becomes the Lords peculiar Subject, Servant, Friend and Son. It would have been presumption in Man to offer this to GOD, Covenants supposing properly equality, freedom from pre-obligations, and Independency between the Parties Covenanting; None of which were, or could be in Covenant-Transactions between GOD and Man, but Infinite distance and Disproportion; Absolute Subjection, Obligation and Dependance on Mans part', under the Dominion and *Law* of his *Creator*, from under which, and without which, it is impossible to conceive he could have a Beeing. But, as it was an Act of Grace and Condescension in GOD, to make Man after His own Image, in perfection of Holiness; So it was an Act of Condescension to illuminate this with the luster of a perfect Law, given for his Rule: Unto this it is a great additament of Condescension, that He should give any promises encouraging to Obedience: And greater, to conceive these confirmed by an Oath. But that the Lord should offer to Covenant with Man, and to give the Law, Promises and Oath Covenant-wayes, is a greater wonder of Condescension: This being a greater priviledge, as well as security, than either Law, Promises or Oaths. This was a wonderful act of Grace and Condescension to Man at first, or the first Man representing all Mankind to propose to him, and to take him under the bond of the Covenant of Works: But after the violation of that first Covenant, that there should be any access granted to any of the Children of Men, to the benefit of a second Transaction of Grace, is a wonder of Condescension never enough considered. The first was the honour and happiness of the first Man, proposed for the benefit, and being violate, became the Shame and Curse of all Men. The second is the honour and happiness,

A　　　　　　　　　　　　　　　　　　　　　　　in

in and through CHRIST, common and peculiar to all the Elect, the Objects of the *Covenant of Redemption*, of which that of Grace is an exhibited Tranfumpt. This being the main difference between the *Eternal Covenant of Redemption* between the Father and the Son, and the *Everlafting Covenant of Grace*, made alfo with CHRIST principally as Reprefentative of His Heirs of Grace and Glory, that in the former, CHRIST our Sponfor is to be confidered, as the Son and fecond Perfon of the *Trinity*, Co-equal and Co-effential with the Father, tranfacting about His Mediatory Delegation in the buffinefs of Redemption; in the later He is to be confidered as the Mediator, the Fathers Servant and Delegate. In the former the Promifes are made conditionally to CHRIST; upon condition of His fatisfying Juftice in the fulnefs of time, and abfolutly to the Elect, without refpect to any thing forefeen in them; in the later they are made abfolutly to Chrift, now having fulfilled His undertaking, and conditionally; or by way of Teftamentary difpofition to the Elect. But as GODS making Covenant with Man is a wonder of never enough admired Condefcendency; fo His admitting Men to make a Covenant with him, is no lefs matter of Admiration. Yet this he hath not only offered and allowed, but perfwaded unto it by Commands, Promifes, Threatnings, Arguments, Expoftulations, Invitations and Intreaties in the Scriptures of the Old and New Teftament: Where we find Covenanting with GOD, both Perfonal and National, hath the fanction of Divine Approbation. For Perfonal Covenanting with GOD, it may be proven by Scripture Precepts, Promifes, and Practifes of the Saints. All thefe Commands and Calls given to come and buy the Covenants Benefits (which fuppofes a *Bargain*) to come to the Marriage &c. inferring a confent to the Terms of a conjugal Covenant, do prove it to be a neceffary Duty. All thefe Promifes of fubfcribing with the hand unto the Lord, *Ifa.* 44. 5. That they fhall call the Lord their Father, and not turn from Him, *Jer.* 3. 19. That they fhall call him *Ifhi*, and no more *Baali*, *Hof.* 2. 16. That he fhall fay *It is my People*, and they fhall fay *The Lord is my GOD*. *Zeeb.* 13. 9. do clearly imply and infer this. There are alfo Precedents and Examples of the Saints confirming this, fuch as *Jacobs* Vow, *Gen.* 28. 20 to the end, *Davids*, *Pfal.* 16. 2. *Pfal.* 119, 57, 106. *Pfal.* 132. 2. 5. and many others. Upon this ground they took confidence to lay particular claim to the Lord as their own GOD, Saviour and Portion

But our purpofe at prefent is to fpeak of *National Covenanting*. For clearing and vindicating which, it will not be unprofitable to confider what

may

may be gathered from this one place of *Scripture*, the 29*th*. Chapter of *Deuteronomy*, the fulleſt and plaineſt that can be found for this purpoſe; whereof the compendious *Analyſis* may be here offered.

In this *Chapter* we have to conſider, theſe ſix things. 1. The *Inſcription* of the Covenant here Renewed, containing the Divine Preſcription of it, *v.* 1. 2. The *Motives* and Inducements here adduced and preſſed by *Moſes*, to invite and incite the People to Renew the Covenant at this time, from *v.* 2. to *v.* 9. Containing alſo, not obſcurely, their Acknowledgement of the *Breaches* thereof. 3. The extent of the *Obligation* thereof, from *v.* 10. to *v.* 15. 4. The danger of the *Breach* of it, from *v.* 16. to *v.* 19. 5. The Greatneſs and Obſervableneſs of the *Puniſhment* of that Breach, predicted and deſcribed from *v.* 20. to *v.* 28. 6. A Concluſory *Corollary* inferred from all, *v.* laſt.

I. The *Inſcription* in the firſt *Verſe*, doth hold out to us both *Verſ.* 1. the Inſtitution of GOD, the place where, or time when it was Tranſacted, and that this was not the firſt time it had been engaged into, but was here Renewed, *Theſe are the words of the Covenant which the Lord commanded Moſes, to make with the Children of Iſrael in the Land of Moab; beſide the Covenant which he made with them in Horeb.* Whence we may have ground for moving and ſolving ſeveral difficulties.

I. It may be doubted, *If Covenanting with GOD, eſpecially Na-* *Queſt.* 1. *tional, be a neceſſary or expedient Duty, approven in the Scriptures?* *Anſ.* The Lawfulneſs of Oaths, Vows, and Covenants, to, for, or before GOD, will be queſtioned by none but *Quakers*, and other *Enthuſiaſts*, or *Fanaticks*. In the Old Teſt. it is here evident the Lord Commanded to enter into this Covenant and Oath *v.* 1. and 12. And it is never Abrogate in the New Teſt. except in ordinary Communications, wherein it was condemned in the Old, as well as in the New. And it is ſo far from being Abrogate, that it is Confirmed by the Apoſtle, ſaying, *A Mans Covenant once confirmed cannot be diſanulled, Gal.* 3. 15. And concerning even Promiſſory Oaths, ſaying, That *an Oath for confirmation is an end of all ſtrife*, Heb. 6. 16. Nor can the expediency or the neceſſity of this Duty be doubted by any who conſiders the Commands enforcing it, the uſefulneſs that the Saints experienced in it, for reſtraining from Sin, for Aggravating it in their Humiliations, from this conſideration, That they had Vowed and Covenanted to the contrary, for ſtirring up to the Duties bound upon them by the Law, and for encouraging themſelves in the hope of Pardon for their Short-comings: We muſt not think it is inconvenient to Vow, or that it is indifferent to Vow, or not Vow.

It

It is said indeed *Ecclef.* 5. 5. *Better it is that thou fhouldeft not Vow, than that thou fhouldeft Vow and not pay.* But that does not make Vowing either Inconvenient, Inexpedient, nor Indifferent, or not good fimply; No more than the Apoftles faying, 2 *Pet.* 2. 21. *It had been better not to have known the way of Righteoufnefs, than after it is known, to turn from it,* will make knowing *the way of Righteoufnefs,* to be either Inconvenient, or Inexpedient, or not good fimply. For *Vowing,* as well as *Paying* is expreſſly commanded, *Pfal.* 76. 11. And in fome cafes (efpecially in neceſſary things) *Vowing,* and *Breaking,* is better than not *Vowing,* and yet *Breaking* the Law; for the later is two Sins, Omiſſion in not Vowing, and Commiſſion in Breaking, the former only the fin of Breaking the Vow, as Mr *Durham* clears it at large, on Command. 3. Pag. 135, 136. &c. 2. As for National Vowing or Covenanting, it is evidently approven in Scripture Precepts, Promifes, and Practifes. Here is a Scripture *Precept* for it in the Old Teſt. never Abrogated in the New. There are alſo *Promifes* and thefe relating to the New Teſt. times, not only of Perſonal, but of National Covenanting; as Churches, and Chriſtian Societies, *Ifa.* 19. 18, 21, 23. to the end. *Jer.* 50. 4. 5. *Zech.* 2. 11. And as for *Precedents;* we have very many of National Covenants, made and renewed again and again; for Prefervation and Reformation of Religion, Extirpation of falfe Worfhip, maintaining their Laws, Liberties, and Government, punifhing and reſtraining the Wicked, keeping the common Peace and mutual Defence, againſt the common Enemies. As here, after that in *Horeb, Ifraels* Covenant is folemnly Sworn, under the Conduct of *Mofes.* And Renewed by *Jofhua, Joſh.* 24. By *Afa,* 2 *Chren.* 15. 13, 14. *Jehojadah,* 2 *Kings* 11. 17. 2 *Chron.* 23. 16. *Hezekiah,* 2 *Chron.* 29. 10. *Jofiah,* 2 *Kings* 23. 2. 2 *Chron.* 34. *Ezra chap.* 10. 3. *Nehemiah,* chap. 9. ult. and 10. 28, 29. Yea alwayes in times of Humiliation and intended Reformarion we find they fell about this Duty, *That the Lords fierce Wrath might turn away.* 2 Chron. 29. 10. *To confirm Ifraels hope, Ezra* 10. 1. *Nehem.* 9. ult. As alfo in the New Teſtament fomewhat like this is hinted at, 2 *Cor.* 8. 5. Where the Churches of *Macedonia* gave their own felves to the Lord, and to the Apoftles, which at leaſt implies a *Covenant.*

Queſt. 2. II. It may be queſtioned, *What was the Nature of thefe Covenants at* Horeb, *and of this in* Moab, *and other National Covenants in Scripture ?* Was it a Covenant of Works or of Grace, that was feveral times Renewed ? And do we ſtand bound to them, as the *Ifraelites* then? *Anf.* Thefe Covenants as to their Nature, were neither the Covenant of Works, nor of Grace formally, though matterially partaking of both.

: the fame mutual contracting *Parties*, GOD and Man
to be confidered, not in his Abftract, Singular, Indi-
al Capacity; But as a Member of a Community un-
The fame obligations to all the duties of thefe fore-
Covenants (thô here they are to be taken as Publick
es, in reference to Religion as a publick Intereft) The
certifications of Bleffings and Curfes (here to be un-
ual) With refpect to the *Matter* of them, in the Old
fation, they obliged to the obfervation of the whole
and Ceremonial Law of GOD, as it was then calcu-
Pedagogie ; requiring indeed perfection legal, accord-
: of the Covenant of Works, but admitting Repen-
a Faith, accepting Perfection Evangelical, according
Covenant of Grace. And in the New Teftament
′ oblige to the fame obfervance of the fame Laws that
and of thefe Ceremonial Inftitutions of CHRIST,
in the place of the former Pedagogical and Typical
late to the Meridian of Gofpel Light , Purity and
refpect to the *End*, in both Difpenfations, they had,
fubferviency to the Covenant of Grace, the fame with
Sin, to manifeft it, and to lead to CHRIST for Re-
with refpect to the feveral *forts* of People engaging
they were to Believers, according to the Tenor of
race ; and to Unbelievers, according to the Tenor of
orks. But as to their *Form* and Formality, they were
d National Covenants of the vifible Community of
engaging to be His, and to keep His Wayes and
t Tranfacted *Exod.* 19. 5, 8. *Exod.* 24. 7, 8. Re-
29. and feveral times afterwards.
eftion is, *Who may tender or impofe it ?* May it *Queft.* 3.
rate ? Here the Magiftrate *Mofes* is Autho-
But *may it be done without him ?* Or when it is fo, *is the*
s, when the Magiftrate or publick Father difallowes or dif-
fon of the doubt is taken from *Numb.* 30. 3, 5, 8.
a Woman in her Fathers houfe (or Husbands) vow
′d, and her Father (or Husband) difallow her, not any
ids, wherewith fhe hath bound her Soul, fhall ftand,
none effect. *Anf.* Juftice and Order requires. that
reateft Influence upon, or Authority over the Community,

munity fhould tender the Oath, and it belongs indeed to Magiftrates to enjoyn it, but not fo as to exclude themfelves from coming under the Bond of it; And in that cafe, they muft have fome to tender it to them. we find the Officers of the Church (as *Mofes* alfo was an extraordinary one) impofing it, as *Jebojadah*, both to King *Joafh* and to the People, 2 *Kings* 11.17. 2 *Chron.* 23. 16. a precedent juftifying Mr *Robert Douglafs,* by Commiffion from the *Gen. Affembly,* his tendering the Covenant to King *Charles* the II. at his Coronation. And *Ezra* made the Priefts, the Levites, and all *Ifrael* to fwear it; and it was acknowledged that *this matter belonged unto him. Ezra* 10. 4, 5. even without the confent of the Magiftrate, or him to whom they were fubjeĉt at that time, then a Hea- then, the King of *Perfia*. And if it be fo tendered and taken, without the confent of the Magiftrate; yet his after diffent or difcharge, cannot loofe the obligation of it. As to that of *Numb.* 30. It is altogether befide the purpofe: For the Magiftrate is neither the Father nor Husband of the Church, thô in fome fenfe *to* the Church, *Ifa.* 49. 23. having a power as a *nurfing* Father, not as a *generating* Father, *Comulative* net *Pri- vative*: Nor hath he fuch power over his Subjeĉts, as a Father over his Child, or Husband over his Wife. Certainly thefe heads of Tribes *verf.* 1. were Politick Fathers, as Magiftrates; yet it is not allowed to them to Difanul, Vacate, or make void thefe Vows, but to the Father or Hus- band of the Party making them, from whom, thefe heads of Tribes are fpoken to, as diftinĉt; and the command is given to thefe Magi- ftrats only to fee it obferved and ratified. Again, National Covenants for Religious Ends and Interefts, are not to be fuppofed of that nature of thefe Vows, which were not about neceffary, but indifferent things, and it feems rafhly and unadvifedly engaged into; for the Father had no power to make null, or of no effeĉt, the Maids engagements to ne- ceffary and indifpenfable Duties. And as to thefe things which he might difallow and difanul, it is faid, *The Lord fhall forgive her,* intimating there was fomething in`quous in it. However, as the Father holding his Peace, did ratifie the Vow. *verfe* 4, and was not to refcind it afterwards, *verfe* 15. So this *Achillean* Argument of the Prelatical and Malignant Party, againft our Covenants adduced from this place, hath no Nerves; becaufe the Father, as they fenfe it, or the Magiftrate held his peace at, and gave his confent to the Renewing both the National Covenant, and Solemn League and Covenant, thô afterwards he made Inquiries, *Prov.* 20. 25. and refcinded it, by an audacious Heaven-daring Law. But dare thefe *Gentlemen* fay, that it was in the power of fuch a politick Father

as

as *Ahaz*, or *Joash*, or *Jeconiah*, or *Zedekiah*, who after Vows made Inquiry, to difallow or difanul the Covenant of *Israel*, and yet it was without their confent, and againſt their will that any ſuch Covenant was made, being made in their Minority, or in their extremity, when forced to it.

A Fourth *Queſtion* may be, *If the Covenant be to be Renewed,*   Queſt. 4. *in what form? Whether in the firſt unalterably? Or may it be Renewed with Alterations? Anſ.* As it is plain here is ſomeway another Covenant, *beſide the Covenant which he made with them in Horeb;* So it is as evident, it is rather a Renovation of the former, than a Subſtitution of another; rather a Tranſlation of the Form, than of the Matter, with accommodation to the Circumſtances, Sins and Duties of that time, *when they were in the Land of Moab,* ſomeway altered from the caſe they were in at *Horeb:* Which were the Motives of their Renewing it at this time, and may conduce for our direction at other times, when to Renew National Covenants. For then at *Horeb,* they were newly delivered out of *Egypt,* and had ſeen the Wonders done there, and at the *Red ſea,* and in conducting them to *Horeb.* Now after their abuſe of theſe, and many ſuperadded Priviledges afterwards, after they had gone through the weary *Wilderneſs,* they were arrived at the Borders of *Canaan,* and put in expectation of the complement of their promiſed Deliverance, when they were to receive, and did receive from the Lord right Judgements, true Laws, good Statutes and Commandements Covenant wiſe, with alluring Propoſalls, that if they would obey His Voice, and keep His Covenant, then He would make them His peculiar Treaſure, and a Kingdom of Prieſts, and an holy Nation, *Exod.* 19. 5. *&c.* Now they had forſaken, broken, and forgotten in a great meaſure this Covenant. Then they were ſolemnly adopted into a Covenant relation with GOD, to be His People; Now they had made Apoſtaſie and Defection, in many reſpects. In a word, they had received many more Mercies, and had committed many more Sins, now, then at that time. Therefore it was expedient they ſhould Renew it: And it is eaſie to obſerve ſeveral Alterations as to the Form of it, from that in *Horeb, Exod.* 19 and *Exod.* 24. 3, 7. The former was more full and particular, ſuiting all times. The *Book of the Covenant* contained all the Judgements promulgated upon Mount *Sinai:* This, as here Renewed, did alſo contain the ſame, but more generally propoſed, with a particular Acknowledgement of the Sins againſt, and Breaches of that Covenant, from *verſe* 2. to 9. and with a new Engagement to the Duties thereof, and a more

expreſs.

exprefs explication and application of the univerfality and extent of its
Obligation : As we find likewife in all the Renovations of the Covenant,
of *Ifrael* formerly mentioned. Which makes it lawful for a People that,
would now Renew *Scotlands* Covenants, to do it with fuitable explicati-
ons and applications to the times.

II. The following part of the *Chapter*, from *verfe* 2, to *verfe* 9, doth
hold forth to us, both their *Acknowledgement of Sins* introductory, and
their *Motives* inducing to take on new *Engagements*.

Queft. 5.   Queft. *What may be the Motives to Renew the Covenant ?*
       Anf. 1. The firft thing here is the confideration of the Won-
ders of Wifdom, Faithfulnefs, Power, Juftice, and Goodnefs of the
Lord, appearing in their Deliverance out of *Egypt*, which they had feen
      done before their Eyes, *v.* 2. The great *Temptations* where-
Verf. 2. 3. with He proved their Faith, Patience, Humility and Love,
      and the great *Temptations* wherewith they provoked Him to
Anger, the *Signs* of His prefence, protection and power continued, many
great *Miracles* wrought in their behalf, notwithftanding of all thefe Temp-
tations, *v.* 3. Which confideration fhould exceedingly aggravate their
Sins, or their *Acknowledgement*, and animate their Zeal in taking on new
Engagements, This alfo may be a *Motive* to the Godly in *Scotland* to Renew their Covenant with GOD, with humble acknowledgement of the
Breaches thereof, aggravated from all the wonderful appearances of
GOD, in ordinances and providences, both of Judgement and Mercy,
wherewith this poor place of the world hath been fignalized beyond o-
thers. We are called to remember *what the Lord did*, in delivering this
Land from the darknefs of *Paganifme*, *Popery* and *Prelaey*, how early He
planted a Church in this Land, how purely He purged it, with what
purity of Reformation, and unity of Profeffion He beautified it, with
what excellent Priviledges He honoured it, efpecially in bringing it under the Bond of Solemn Covenants ; whereby its Name became *Beulah*
and *Hephzibah*, and what excellent Teftimonies for CHRIST's Prerogatives as King, and His Kingdoms Liberties, He did concredit to it,
to contend for. Our eyes alfo, and our Fathers have feen *great Tempta-*
tions in Providences, whence we might have learned great experiences
of the Lords Wifdom and our folly: Alwayes when we were at the low-
eft extremity, difpairing in our felves, then He appeared in Mercy: Alwayes when we thought our felves ftrongeft, and were moft confident
in our felves, then we were confounded. The Lords Temptations to
try us have been manifold, and our Tentations to provoke Him, have
                                                              been

been as multifarious. The *Signs* and *Miracles* in the conduct of His Providences, in this day of Tentation, have been observable : As *Israel* in the Wilderness, so we have had our *Mara's*, and our *Massa's*, and *Meriba's* *Taberahs*, and *Kibroth Hattaavahs*, at *Pentland* hills, *Bothwel bridge*, *Airdsmoss*, &c. But above all, the passages of Providence since the late *Popish King* mounted the Throne, raised up wonderfully for our scourge, have been wonderful, both for the manner of his Advancement and subsequent Emergencies. After all the former breakings, two Parties in both Kingdoms appearing against him, very seasonally, when it would have been thought all would have concurred and concerted the same Cause against *Popery* and *Tyranny*, yet were broken: And nothing was like to withstand his designs of introducing the blackest of *Popery* & basest of Slavery, at the opened Gap of the *Tolleration*, had not a Forreign *Prince*, in Zeal for Religion, Pity to these Lands, and in pursuit of his own Right, interposed for our rescue, by a very propitious providence; which, in a way as of Signs and Miracles, hath given us this enlargement and reviving in our Bondage. Shall not therefore the Godly from these considerations, be stirred up both to Acknowledgements of Sins and new Engagements.

2. The consideration of their Obduration, Occecation and *Verf.* 4. Obstinacy, supine Stupidity, and unanswerableness to these great Miracles and Mercies forementioned, which they had neither gotten Hearts to perceive, nor Eyes to observe, *verse* 4. is both a Motive to their acknowledgement of Sins, and to their engagement to covenanted Duties. As this is a sad truth, as suitably applicable to *Scotland*, as to *Israel*; so the consideration thereof, should have moved the Godly to renew their Acknowledgements and Covenants, if yet they had gotten Hearts to perceive, and Eyes to see &c. Alas! all the pains the Lord hath taken on us to reclaim and reforme us, have not profited us, Priviledges have not prevailed with us, Prosperity hath not allured us, Adversity hath not awakened us to our duty, and all the fruit and effect of the Word and Works of God, seems to have produced nothing but the judicial Plague of *hearing indeed , but not understanding ; seeing indeed, but not perceiving ; and making our heart fat,* &c. Isa. 6. 9. 10. Is it not time then we were considering our wayes, and turning to the Lord, and Covenanting with Him.

3. The consideration of the Lords gracious Conduct of *Verf.* 5. 6. them in the *Wilderness* fourty Years, providing them with all necessaries for Food & Cloathing, thô in an extraordinary way, wherein they

they might know the care and kindnefs of , and their relation to the Lord their God, *verf.* 5.6. is made ufe of as a Motive to induce them to Acknowledgement of their Sins, and a new Eugagement to the duties of their Covenant. Since our Covenants were renewed in *Scotland*, with a Solemn Acknowledgement of the Sins, and Engagements to the duties thereof, the Lord hath led us full 40 Years through the wildernefs of the *Seɛtarian* Invafions, and the *Prelatick*, *Eraftian*, and *Antichriftian* Ufurpations: Wherein, thô we did not meet with Miracles, yet truly we have experienced Wonders of the Lords care and kindnefs, and for all the Haraffings and Huntings, Spoilings and Depredations of Perfecuters, the poor Wildernefs-wanderers have looked as Meat-like and Cloath-like (as we ufe to fay) as others that fat at eafe in their houfes, and drank their Wine and their ftrong drink.

Verf. 7. 8. 4. The confideration of the glorious Viɛtory obtained in this place, in the Land of *Moab*, over the King of *Hefhbon*, and the King of *Bafhan*, who withftood their progrefs unto the *Reft* they were feeking, whofe Lands fell unto the two Tribes and the half for an Inheritance, *verf.* 7. 8. is likewife adduced as an Argument to excite them to this duty. So in our day, the Trophees of Triumph, that the late revolutions of Providence have.ereɛted, to the Honour of our God, and the advantage of the Covenanted Reformation, in removing out of the way, two *Kings*, that were withftanding its propagation, and feeking its deftruɛtion; and in abolifhing two wicked Eftablifhments, fet up on the ruines thereof, viz. *Tyranny in the State*, and *Prelacy in the Church*, may ftir up all Lovers of Reformation to the fame duty of Covenanting, for its Reftauration and Prefervation.

Verf. 9. 5. Finally, he moves them to it *verf. 9.* by a promife of profperity to enfue upon their keeping and doing this Covenant, which now they were about to Renew. Which he preffes as neceffary duty, from all thefe Confiderations.

Queft. 6. It may be *Queftioned* here. *What is it to keep the words of the Covenant, and do them?* Is any Man able to keep the Covenant, more than the Command ? *And if not, why is this further burden impofed, are not the Commands themfelves Bonds ftriɛt enough? An.* The Covenant is kept and done. (1.) By a conftant and fuitable Profeffion of the duties thereof, keeping the way of the Lord. (2.) By a tenacious Confeffion of the Teftimonies thereof, againft all oppofition, never denying or forbearing the afferting the obligation thereof, nor turning afide therefrom, to the right hand or to the left (*Jofh.* 23.6) keeping it without fpot, unrebukable

able (1 *Tim.* 6. 14.) especially when it becomes the word of His Patience, *Rev.* 3. 10. (3.) By a mindful & careful entertainment of it in the mind and memory, never forgetting what we are bound to thereby. (4.) By a strict observance thereof in the practise, in all manner of conversation. Which is to be understood in the Gospel sense, not absolutely but respectively, with respect to our Nature, now corrupt, weak and perverse. For though we be bound by the Law of God to be perfectly Holy, yet our Covenants do not tye us to this perfection; and this obligation is not from our Covenant, but from the Law; for our Covenants do not oblige to the victory over all sin, but to wrestle for it; not to the event, but to the means which are in our power (and therefore the People of God plead they had not broken Covenant, *Pfal.* 44. 17. thô they had sins) and not to the attaining all things we Covenant for, but to the aim, desire, design and endeavour, to live in no sin Covenanted against, never to approve our selves in it, to omit no known duty engaged unto, and to leave no mean unessayed for attaining the whole of it. See Mr *Durham* on 3 *Command.* concerning the obligation of Vowes, Page 133. &c.

III. In the following words from *verf.* 10. to *verf.* 15, or 17. *Moses* proposes the matter more closely, shewing the extant of the obligation thereof, in a threefold respect· 1. In respect of the Universality of the Persons obliged. 2. In respect of the sacredness and inviolable strictness of its Obligation 3. In respect of the perpetuity of its Obligation.

First, In respect of the Persons obliged, it is of universal extent, binding and obliging all the Members of the Church, and Common-wealth of *Israel* of all sorts, *qualities, ranks, vocations, ages, sexes,* none excluded for these things. 1. All of all qualities, *Captains, Elders* or *Verf.* 10. Magistrates, *Officers,* both of Church and State, with *all the Men of Israel.* Accordingly we find *Josiah* taking all engaged, all the Men of *Judah,* and the Priests and the Prophets and all the People both small and great, 2 *Kings* 23. 2. And *Ezra* made the chief Priests and Levites, and all *Israel* to swear the Covenant, *Ezra* 10. 5. None are so high that they are above the obligation of it; None so small or base that they are below it. Its very encouraging when there are Nobles and Captains &c. to take the Covenant. Its very necessary they should go before others in it, but it does not only belong to them.

Quer. *May the Covenant be renewed without thefe* Captains, *Quest.* 7. Elders, Officers, *or* Primores & Primates Regni, *when they will not concur?* *Anf.* Certainly this extensive obligation reaching all Persons,

is

(12)

is to be underſtood *poſitively*, that all theſe are obliged to enter into Covenant, but not *negatively*, that without any of theſe, the Govenant ſhould
not be entered into. The Motives mentioned are common to the ſmal,
as well as the great, and without them, as well as with them, the Articles of it, and the keeping and doing them are common to both alike :
The relation that the ſmal and meaner ſort of People have to God (the
other contracting party) is the ſame that the Nobles and Great-ones
have, *verf. 12.* and the Priviledges of it, to be eſtabliſhed as a People unto
Himſelf, and to have him for their God, *verf. 13.* do no more belong
to the one, than to the other ; and conſequently the Smal may renew it
as well as the Great, but not Nationally, to bind the whole Nation formally, to which indeed the concurrence of its Repreſentatives is neceſ-
Verf. 11.   ſary. 2. All of all Ages and Sexes, even their *Little-ones* and their
         Wives, verf. 11. are obliged to take it, if they be capable. Con-
Queſt. 8. cerning which, Quer. *If Children may be admitted to the Covenant?*
         Anf. It cannot be doubted but they are under the bond of it
materially, being Children of the Covenant *Ad. 3. 25.* to whom belong
the promiſes (and alſo the duties how ſoon they are capable) of the Covenant of Grace *Ad. 2. 29.* and that they are obliged to take it if they
be capable ; otherwiſe their Parents are to engage for them. Accordingly in *Scotland* it hath been in uſe for faithful Miniſters to take Parents engaged to the *covenants* when they preſented their Children to Baptiſm. 3.
Queſt. 9. All of all ranks or *relations, even Strangers & Servants, from the bew-
         er, of wood, to the drawer of water.* Quer. *If Strangers be obliged, or to be
admitted to the Covenant ? Anf.* As in *Iſrael,* Strangers being admitted to the
covenant, together with their *circumciſion* was one bage of their being *proſely-
tes* (of which Strangers only this is to be underſtood) ſo now, thô the caſe
differ very far, ſuch *ſtrangers as are naturalized* and *reſide* in the *country,* may
be admitted to the National Covenant of that Nation whereof they are
ſubjects, and wherein they are Church Members : Others are only to
be reſtrained from doing or ſaying any thing againſt it. 4. Neither only theſe that ſtood there before the Lord in that place, but the abſent
Queſt. 10. alſo *verf. 13. 14.* Some might have had as good reaſon then
         to *Object,* as many do now fooliſhly, that perſonally *they never
took the Covenant,* being not preſent when it was taken. But it is plain here,
abſence will not abſolve from the obligation of it ; ſo it is in all real Covenants, that are not meerly Perſonal. All the Members of the Community covenanting are under the bond of the common Covenant. It
would be a ridiculous exception for one to alledge, they are not obliged to ſtand to the Allegiance ſworn to a King, or to a Covenant of Peace
                                                                made

madé with an Independant Nation by the Community of that Nation, whereof they are Members, becaufe they were abroad when thefe Tranfactions were made. But with reference to all thefe it may be a *Queftion, May the Covenant univerfally be impofed upon all ranks and forts of Perfons?* Or, *May all be admitted to take it?* Anf. Thô all be *Queft.* II. under the obligation of it *materially*, and all are bound to take it *formally*, *ceteris paribus*, if they be qualified; yet neither ought it to be impofed, nor fhould any be admitted but with refpect to their capacities Gracious and Legal. The *Wicked*, that are fcandalous and obftinate in Wickednefs, Error, Profanity or Malignancy, hating Inftruction, and cafting the Lords Word behind them, have not Gods right to it, for unto fuch He faith, *what haft thou to do to take up my Covenant in thy mouth.* Pfal. 50. 16, 17. Some were legally incapacitate, as the Enemies of Truth and Godlinefs, with whom they were not to affociate, *Exod.* 23. 31. Exod. 34. 15. *Deut.* 7. 2. *Judg.* 2. 2. *Ezra* 4. 3. *Ezra* 9. 14. Who is to be underftood with this exception, except they were Profelytes and Penitents fuch as *Rabab*, *Joſh.* 2. It is clear from the Scriptures thô all are bound to it, it is to be impofed upon and tendered to none but thofe that fubfcribe to it with choife and refolution, *Joſh.* 24. 15. 22. None but fuch as are reformed from the Defections and Complyancies of the time, *Neh.* 10. 28. None but fuch as have knowledge and underftanding of the Sins and Duties contained in the Covenant- *ibid.* None but fuch as can fwear and fubfcribe it according to thefe qualifications of an Oath, *Jer.* 4. 2. *in truth in judgement and in righteoufnefs.*

Secondly. The Obligation of this Covenant is fhewed to be *Ver: 12:* very great, not only *extenfively* but *intenfively*, *Verf.* 12. 13. It muft be very facred, inviolable & *ftriciffimi juris*, fince 1. it is a *Covenant* and *Oath* mutually entered into by *Ifrael* with the *Lord* their *God*, and by the *Lord* with *them*, *ver:* 12: and confequently cannot be diffolved but by confent of both Parties.

It is a grave *Queftion, Can nothing loofe the Obligation of a law-* *Queft:* 12: *ful Oath?* *Anfw:* 1. It may be clear enough that thofe things will not, which falfe fwearers pretend; and which they that would caft off the yoke of thefe Covenants do plead fometimes; As no mans temporal lofs or prejudice will make an Oath null, or loofe from the Obligation of it, (though we fwear to our own hurt, we muft not change; *Pfal:* 15: 4:) nor thô the Oath do engage to fomething in its own nature indifferent (for by an Oath, even in things indifferent antecedently, our Souls are bound, *Numb:* 30. 2:) nor the extortion of it by by fear or violence, if the matter be lawful ; nor the deceit and guile of others, if the deceit be circumstantial only, as in that oath to the *Gibeonites*; Nor sinful rashnefs in the manner, if lawful in the matter, as *Joshuahs* oath to the *Gibeonites*. Nor any good meaning or intention in reverfing the oath (*Saul* was punished for *breaking* that oath with the *Gibeonites* many *generations* after, thô he did it out of his zeal to the Children of *Ifrael*, 2 *Sam.* 21: 2:) Nor thô the Oath be conceived by Creatnres (as by the Altar or Temple, Heaven, &c. *Math.* 23. 20, 22.) Nor when the thing becomes impossible, if that impossibility could have been forefeen or prevented. Nor when the condition is unlawful, if already fulfilled (as *Juda's* promifing a Kid to *Thamar*) Nor another meaning afterwards devifed, nor according to the Impofers mind , nor our own at firft who took it (that's but a fwearing *deceitfully Pfal.* 24:4;) Nor any other fecret meaning by Equivocation, or mental Refervation; Nor any Difpenfation from *Pope* or *King*. None of thefe things can make an Oath void, bnt if we have bound our felves, God will require it, for whofo defpifeth an Oath by breaking the Covenant *when lo he hath given his hand*, he fhall not efcape, *Ezek.* 17. 18, 19. God will recompence it. But (2) Oaths have no force, when the thing fworn is finful and unlawful in it felt: Or unlawful to him that fweareth : Or fimply impoffible : Or when the thing fworn is not in our own power, *Numb.* 30. 5. Or when there is deceit in it, not in Circumftantials, but in Effentials: Or when it hinders a greater good : Or when the cafe materially altereth: Or when the party fworn to relaxeth us. In which refpefts the third Article of the *Solemn League and Covenant* did not oblige us to owne the Authority of Tyrants and Ufurpers when reigning over us, becaufe in that cafe the obligation was unlawful, and there was a deceit in Effentials, puting in Tyranny for Authority, and the cafe materially altered (we being bound in the Covenant to a King or Magiftrate defendiug Religion and Liberty, not to a Tyrant overturning thefe) and the party fworn to had relaxed us long ago by refcinding the Covenants. But none of all thefe things can any way enervate the facred Obligation of *Scotlands* Holy *Covenants* with God, which ftill muft ftand in inviolable force.

2. The Covenants Obligation muft be very facred and ftrong, fince it is propofed for fuch *gracious ends*, &in order to enfure fuch *glorious priviledges*, *ver: 13:* which are two or three, *ver:* 13: refpefting the *muiual ftipulation* of the Parties contrafting (1)*That he might eftablifh them that day for a people unto Himfelf.* To be eftablifhed a people unto the Lord not only by *creation*, which is common to all ; or *Profeffion*, which is common to

the

the *Church visible* , but by *Covenant engagement* to be His and for Him, is both the *Lords end*, and should be ours in publick or personal Covenanting. And it is a very *glorious priviledge* to be His people in a peculiar manner, of whom He will take particular notice and inspection , and who have a'nearer relation to Him than other people. As likewise, it is the great duty of *Covenanters* to avouch themselves to be his people, to walk in His wayes, keep His statutes, and hearken to His voice, *Deut: 26: 16, 17, 18.* which is the comprehensive *stipulation* of all Covenants with GOD. (2.) *And that He might be unto them a GOD,* not only by universal *Dominion,* nor only by *Redemption,* first by *price,* and then by *power* , but by *Covenant,* is the *Lords end,* our *priviledge* (the greatest of priviledges, Honours and Happinesses, in getting hereby all His *Divine Attributes, Covenant Relations, Mediatory-Offices* , and all that He hath purposed or promised, or *Christ* hath purchased for the good of His people, to be ours ;) And it is the *mutual stipulation* of both parties. The Lord for his part undertakes to be a *God* unto us, and avouch us to be His people ; And we for our part should promise and engage to be His people, and avouch Him to be our *God, Deut. 26 16, 17, 18.* Or as it is, *Zech. 13. ult.* He will say, *it is my people,* and Covenanters will say *the Lord is my God.* (3) And that He might confirm not only what He had said unto them, but what He had *sworn unto their Fathers.* This is the Lords *End* in all Covenants which He ownes with His People, that by two immutable things in which it is impossible for *God* to lie, they may have strong Consolation, *Heb. 6: 18:* having such ample security to repose their confidence upon : This is the *priviledge* of his Covenanted People, to have not only the *Lords word* for their security, but his *Oath* , confirmed by *Covenant,* which not only they, but their Fathers before them did experience, that He did constantly keep, verifie and fulfill. And as here, He undertakes to make it good ; so they engage to depend upon it , and to keep what they and their Fathers had said and sworn in point of Obedience. Now in regard of these Ends, Priviledges and Stipulations, the Covenant must have a strict and sacred obligation as inviolable, as we would desire these to be inamissible, or as we would not come short of being a people unto Himself , and having Him for our *God,* as He hath said unto us and sworn unto our Fathers. If the *Question* be then, *What the better shall we be of making and keeping a National Covenant ?* Here is *Quest: 13:* the *Answer,* Here by shall we be established a people unto Himself, and He shall be unto us a *God,* as He hath said and sworn, which comprehends all advantages imaginable.

Thirdly, .

Verf. 14, 15.   *Thirdly,* Here not obfcurely is demonftrated the extent
of the Obligation of this Covenant, in refpect of the *perpetui-
tie* of it. It is a Covenant oblieging not only the prefent, *verf.* 14: but the
abfent, *verf.* 15. And not only the abfent in regard of *place*, but in re-
·gard of *time.* It obliged all the Children of *Ifrael* that were *not there that
day*: Which comprehends not only thofe that were then living, but future Generations. The reafons added do clearly enough confirm this.
1. The probable hazard of Apoftafie and Prefumption in breaking, this
Covenant was perpetual, *verf.* 16, 17, 18, 19 Not only that Generation
that day which came out of *Egypt,* and paffed by the Nations and faw
their Abominations and their Idols, were in hazard of turning away
from the Lord, ferving the gods of the Nations, having among them a
Root bearing Gall and Worm wood, who might blefs themfelves in
their prefumption of Impunity, notwithftanding the threatned curfe. But
much more in after Generations , they that never dwelt in the
Land of *Egypt* (and never faw the plagues punifhing that Lands wickednefs) but afterward might fee the abominations and the *Dungy-gods* (as it
is in the *Hebrew*) of other Nations, were in hazard of that defection and
prefumption, when the Covenant might be worn antiquated, out of date
and mind, which might encourage them (much more than at that time
when it was in every Bodies mouth and memory) to fay *I fhall have peace
thô I walk in the imagination of mine heart.* 2. The threatned punifhment
of the breach of this Covenant was *perpetual.* The Lords anger and jealoufie fhall fmokagainft *Covenant-breakers,* all the Curfes written fhall lye
upon them, their names fhall be blotted out from under Heaven, *verf.*
20. He fhall feparate them unto evil. *verf.* 21. Not only in that age
wherein the Covenant was Renewed, but the Generation to come of
their Children that fhould rife up after them, fhall obferve the punifhment of the Pofterity, when they fhall have forfaken the Covenant of
the Lord God of their Fathers, and the Lord fhall have rooted them
out of their Land for the fame, *verf.* 22. to 28. which was not accompli-
fhed till many Centuries afterwards.

Quefl. 14.   Quer. *If the Obligation of National Covenants, where the matter is
lawful, be perpetual and binding upon Pofterity ? Anfw.* If any
Engagements can be fuppofed binding to Pofterity, certainly National
Covenants to keep the Commandments of *God,* and to adhere to his inftitutions, muft be of that nature. It cannot be denyed that feveral O-
bligations do bind Pofterity. Publick *Promifes,* with annexation of curfes
to the breakers, make the Pofterity obnoxious, as well as thofe who per.
fonally

fonally came under the Engagement, *Neh:* 5: 12, 13: That promise of the *Jewish* Nobles and Rulers would have brought their Posterity under the Curse, if they had exacted usury of their Bretheren, as *Joshua's* Adjuration did oblige all posterity never to build *Jericho, Josh. 6. 26,* and the breach of it did bring the Curse upon *Hiel* the *Bethelite* in the dayes of *Ahab.* Publick *Vowes* do bind Posterity, *Jacobs* Vow *Gen. 28. 21.* did oblige all his posterity, virtually comprehended in him, *Hof. 12. 4.* The *Rechabites* found themselves obliged to observe the Vow of their Fore-father *Jonadab, Jer. 35. 6. 14.* Publick *Oaths* do oblige posterity, *Joseph* took an Oath of the Children of *Israel* to carry up his Bones to *Cannan, Gen. 50. 25.* which did oblige the posterity some hundreds of years after, *Exod. 13 19. Josh. 24. 32.* National *Covenants* with *Men* before *God,* do oblige posterity, as *Israels* Covenant with the *Gibeonites, Josh. 9. 15. 19:* for the breach whereof, many Ages after, the posterity was plagued, 2 *Sam. 21. 1.* So *Zedekiab's* Covenant with *Nebuchadnezzar, Ezek. 17. 18, 19.* Especially National Covenants with *God* before Men, about things Moral, Objectively obliging, are Perpetual, *Jer. 50. 5.* And yet more especially (as *Grotius* observes) when they are of an Hereditary nature, that is, when the subject is permanent, the matter Moral, the end Good, and in the form of them there is a Clause expressing their perpetuity. All which Ingredients of perpetual Obligations are clear in *Scotlands* Covenants: Which are National *Promises,* adjuring all the Members of the *Scottish* Church, under a Curse to preserve and promote Reformation, according to the Word of *God,* and to extirpate what is in Doctrine, Worship, Discipline or Government opposite thereto: National *Vowes,* devoting the then engaging and succeeding Generations to be the Lords people, and to walk in His wayes: National *Oaths,* solemnly sworn by all Ranks, with hands lifted up to the Most High GOD, never to admit of Innovations, or submit to Usurpations contradictory to the Word of *God:* National *Covenants* wherein the King, Parliament, and People did Covenant with each other, to perform their repective duties, in their several places and stations, inviolably to preserve Religion and Liberty: Yea National *Lawes,* solemnly ratified by King and Parliament, and made the foundation of the Peoples Compact with the King at his Inauguration: And Finally, they are National Covenants with *God* as party contracting, to keep and do the Words of His Covenant. The *subject* or parties contracting are permanent, as long therefore as *Scotland* is *Scotland,* and *God* is Unchangeable, who hath given His revealed Will for the Rule of Mans Obedience, *Scotlands* Reformation in Doctrine, Wor-

C   ship,

ſhip, Diſcipline and Government, muſt be endeavo
in a conformity to it. The *Miner* of them is moral,
but what is antecedently and eternally binding, all
been a formal Covenant, The *Ends* of them perpe
For defence of the true Religion, as it was then reformed,
Confeſſion of Faith, and *which hath been* for many years, with
preached and profeſſed in this Kirk and Kingdom, as God's w
ed only upon His written Word. And for maintaining the
ſon and Eſtate &c. Having before our eyes the Glory of
ment of the Kingdom of our Lord Jeſus Chriſt, the honou
Kings Majeſty, and his Poſterity, and the true publick Li
of the Kingdoms, wherein every ones private condition is i
very Forme of them, there are Clauſes expreſſing
in that Article of the *National Covenant*, ſubſcribed
theſe words, *Being convinced in our minds, and confeſſing*
the preſent and ſucceeding Generations in this Land, are b
National Oath and Subſcription inviolable. In the Solem
That we and our poſterity after us may as brethren live in l
Lord may delight to dwell in the midſt of us. *Art.* 5. We
may remain conjoined in a firm Peace and Union, to all p

    IV. Next, from *verſ.* 16. to 20. Th
Verſ. 16. 17. warns, that, and all Generations, of t
Covenant. Shewing, *Firſt*, The Inductives to thi
to the danger of it, and involving them in the gu
before them what ſhall be the puniſhment of it.

    If it be enquired then , *What are*
Queſt. 15. inducing to this ſin of Covenant-breaking ? I
Dwelling among , and converſe with a People o
ye know how ye have dwelt in the Land of Egypt. --- and
nations &c. (as it is noted in a *Parentheſis, v.* 16, 17
Perſons, Families and Tribes, *verſ* 18. (and in th
then Families, then Tribes) to ſymbolize with th
are more readily ſeduced to ſin, by the perverſe
live among, than they can be induced to abide ir
ſtructions of thoſe that watch over them. No
dwelling among Infidels, be in hazard of ſeducti
tollerated to dwell among the Lords people, wil
therefore is that command given, *Exod.* 23. *ult.* They
leſt they make thee ſin againſt me. The example of t

Malignant faction in *Brittain* and *Ireland*, the suffering them not only to dwell, but to creep into places of Power and Trust in *Scotland*, after they were once in a good meafure expelled; And efpecially, in procefs of time, the ftupid fubmiffion to theReftitution of their Government of Church and State, and to the Re-introduction of their wicked Eftablifhments, abjured by Covenant, and to the impofition of wicked Laws contrary to the Covenant, did gradually induce, firft particular perfons among us, then whole Families, after that Tribes, Parifhes and Provinces, to this dreadful fin of Covenant-breaking.

2. Heart defection, *The heart turning away from the Lord, ver.* 18. *Verf.* 18. is the firft ftep to external defection, in Profeffion, Practife or Principle, from the Covenant of God, *The back-flider in Heart fhal be filled with his own way. If any Man draw back the Lord will have no Pleafure in him;* and then he is Plagued with Hardnefs of Heart, and Blindnes of mind, to run upon fins againft the Covenant of God, not for feeing nor fearing the curfe of it. The Lords People in *Scotland*, turned firft away from the Lord in Heart, fell from their *firft Love*, Livelinefs, Tendernefs, Sincerity and Fervor in Heart Religion, and then they could not but be a Prey to the tentations of the time, the wicked Examples and Laws, drawing and driving to Covenant breaking.

3. Inclinations to Idolatry of any fort, *To go and ferve the gods of thefe Nations. ver.* 18. Idolatry is a breach of Covenant, and inclination to it does eafily infnare in the guilt of it. Where a man begins once whorifh-ly to look after idols of any kind ; he is readily and righteoufly left to follow his look. Not only is it Idolatry to worfhip Wood and Stone, Silver and Gold, but to give Gods due to any other Object (contrair to the 1ft: *Command;*) And to worfhip Him any other way then he hath commanded (contrair to the 2d: *Command;*) There are many *heart idols*, as *Self, theWorld, &c. Covetoufnefs* being Idolatry. There are many *land-idols* of jealoufie, as when any wicked *Intereft* and *Courfe* is fet up, in competiti-on with, and oppofition to, and complied with in prejudice of Chrifts Intereft and Caufe. Thus in this Land, the Eftablifhment of *Eraftianfifm, Prelacy, Supremacy,* and *Abfolute Power,* afcribing to Kings of Clay, what is the incommunicablePrerogative of the Prince of the Kings of the earth, and Peoples *love of the World, felf peace, eafe, liberty,* &c. Incomplyance with thefe Interefts, have been the *Idols of thefe Nations*: And their heart turning away from the Lord to thefe, have led them to forfake the Covenant.

4. Hereupon follows *the root that beareth Gall and Wormwood, ver.* 19. which is a bribed, blinded, or feared Confcience, or *an evil heart of unbelief*

C 2   in

in departing from the Living God, Heb. 13. 12. *A root of bitternefs springing up*, whereby many are defiled, *Heb.* 12. 15. When the heart turns away from God, then it inclines to Idols : when it is fo bewitched, then the Confcience, that is firft Reclamant, gets a bribe from the perverted will aud affeƈions to hold its peace at, and to excufe fin, and then its diƈtats are *Gall* and *Worm-wood*, being blinded with Error, it feeks arguments to juftify the finful Praƈtice, and at length is fo feared, that it is proof againft all reproof, and wholly benummed with the deceitfulnefs of fin under the energy of ftrong delufions, which are bitter in the end. This hath been the fourth ftep leading in breach of Covenant in *Scotland*; when firft the Tentation was prefented, of bowing to thefe Idols of jealoufie above mentioned , and the *Queftion* ftated, fhall we Comply, or Renounce the Covenant? People firft confulted their own Intereft and Credit , and then when that was determined to be fecured, the Confcience was foon lulled afleep, and perfwaded to applaud the fleſhly conclufion, and then the judgement was fet on work , to find out plaufible Arguments, *and after vows to make inquiry* to get fhifts, excufes and defences for their complyances, and to excogitate pernicious principles about the Magiftrates power in Church affairs, his power in loofing the obligation of Covenants, and the indifferencie of *forms* of Church Government, and the fmalnefs of fuch points to be heads of fuffering, *&c.* to juftifie their breach of Covenant. Thefe *roots* have brought forth the bitter fruits of *gall* and *wormwood*, that have brought this Land under the curfe of the Covenant.

Verfe 19. 5 Secure felf-flattering prefumption, bleffing himfelf and faying, *I fhall have peace, tho I walk in the imagination of my heart, &c. ver.* 19 This is the higheft ftep of preparatives to, and the heinoufeft aggravation of the fin of *perjury*, and the bittereft fruit that grewes from the root of *Apoftacy* from God, including many ingredients of the unpardonable fin, trampling upon *Light*, the prefumer being fuppofed *to hear the words of this curfe*, and to *tufh* at all threatnings, bleffing himfelf in his *deliberate* finning with *delight* , not only *fecurely*, but *felf-willedly*, and refolutely proceeding from evil to worfe, promifing to himfelf *peace*, not only outward, purchafed by refolved perjury, but inward, in the fleep of a *feared confcience*. A man fo far left of *God* , cannot withftand the tentations to Covenant-breaking ; No bonds can reftrain his running head-long down the precipice to deftruƈtion. Yet the full amount of all this prefumption, hath been very frequent in this *apoftatizing Generation* , on the front of whofe perjury and perfidy, in complying with the mifchiefs
framed

Tamed into Laws, by a Throne of iniquity, this *motto* hath been legibly written, *I shall have peace, thô I walk in the imagination of my heart.*

V. From *verse* 20, to 28. the punishment of breach of Covenant is threatned, predicted and described, with reference to a twofold breach of Covenant; procuring a twofold punishment: *personal perjury*, threatned with *personal; National*, with *National judgements.*

First, *Personal perjury* is in two *verses* made obnoxious to ma- *Verse* 20. ry terrible threatnings, every clause thundering vengeance.

If it be asked, *What may every Covenant-breaker expect?* The *Quest.* 16. Spirit of *God* Answers. 1. *The Lord will not spare him.* This is *Meiosis*, importing far more than is expressed, to wit , a threatning of inexorable, ineluctable and irresistible judgement wherein there shall be no allay of Mercy, as *Ezek.* 5. 11. *Ezek.* 7. 4. 9. implying neverthe-less alwayes an exception of Repentance. Otherwise, the Lord will not spare the presumptuous Covenant-breaker , be who he will , be he King or Beggar , Magistrate or Minister, or private Person. 2. *But then the anger of the Lord , and His jealousie shall smoke against that man.* O who can express or conceive the horror of that misery , of being the object of *Divine indignation*, in its full. vigor and rigor, as the *smoking* of it imports? Yet this is the doom of the Apostatizing, presumptuous, self-flatering Covenant-breaker; *Deut:* 31: 16, 17. *They will break my Covenant, then my anger shall be kindled against them in that day, and I will forsake them, and I will hide my face from them, and they shall be devoured, and many evils and troubles shall befal them,* &c. *Josh.* 23. *ult. When ye have transgressed the covenant of the Lord your God, then shall the anger of the Lord be kindled against* us. Mal. 3. 5. The Lord will *come near to judgement*, and will be a *swift witness against false swearers,* &c. 3. *And all the curses that are written in this book shall lie upon him.* All Covenants have a Curse, *Neh.* 10 29. The Curse of this Covenant is some way greater than the Curse of the Law, deserving and procuring the Mediators vengeance, which is a sorer pu. ishment than vengeance of a broken Law, *Heb.* 10 28, 29. Compre-ending all Miseries, Temporal, Spiritual and Eternal. This is the *flying Roll, the length whereof is twenty Cubits, and the breadth thereof ten Cubits, Zech.* 5. 2, 3. 4. We have a black and broad roll of Curses appointed into Covenant-breakers, *Lev.* 26. 15. to the close, Terrers, Consumption, Burning agues, Enemies prevailing, Rage of Tyrants reigning, Bar-nnels of Land, Wild beasts devouring, the raging Sword, Pestilence, Famine, Desolation Faintness, and pining away in Iniquities, &c. And another, may Cubits long and broad, *Deut.* 28. from 15. to the end.

We

We fee what Curfes are threatned againft the M
Covenant, *Jer.* 34. 18, 20. *&c.*. He will give them
Enemies, and into the hand of them that feek th
15, 18, 19. *Shall be profper? fhall he efcape? fhall h*
be delivered? feing he defpifed the Oath, by breaking th
had given his hand? he fhall not efcape. As I live, I w
own head. 4. *And the Lord fhall blot out his name fro*
think to efcape by Iniquity, and to purchafe, fom
and reft, but efteem and renown, by perfidious an
ing. And the greateft Complyers, who kept thei
for adhering to the Covenant of *God*, loft or left
that their houfes fhall continue for ever, they call
Names (*Pfal.* 49. 11.) But the Spirit of *God* faith
blotted out, and fhall ftink. *Job.* 18. 17, *Their r*
and they fhall have no name in the ftreet. Job, 20. 7. H
his own dung, they which have feen him, fhall fay, whe
Men fhall clap their hands at him, and fhall bifs him
35. 36. Thô for a time, he may be great in powe
like a green bay tree, yet he fhall pafs away, a
Pfal. 52. 5. 6, 7. He fhall be *pluckt out of his dwellin*
the Land of the Living. The righteous alfo fhall fee and
him. *Lo this is the Man that made not God his ftrength*
dance of his riches, and ftrengthned himfelf in his wicke
name of the wicked fhall rot. Prov. 1 ?. 9. *The lamp of*
Verfe 21. when the light of the Righteous fhal
Lord fhall feparate him unto evil, out of all t
ing to all the Curfes of the Covenant, that are written in t
21. Thô all Sinners are obnoxious, yet in a mo
Covenant-braker fhall be feparate, or fingled out
Indignation and Jealoufie. He fhall particularly
geance. Many evils fhall befal him, efcape who
cording to all the Cu fes of the Covenant, Tem
ternal. He fhall be a prey to all the evils cf fin,
of trouble, and devoted, as a Faggot, for Hells
Secondly, National covenant-breaking, is threatned
judgements, from *verf.* 22. to 28. Wherein, the obfer
greatnefs of them. is not only threatned, but predi
16, 17, *&c.* with the event) and defcribed. St
vers. 2. The thing obferved, or the eccafio

3. Their enquiry upon their observations. 4. Their Answer obvious and ready.

1. The Observers of the Lords Judgements upon the Nation *Verf.* 22 of *Ifrael*, breaking Covenant with *God*, are, *The Generation to come of their Children,* and the *Stranger that shall come from a far Land*, verf. 22. Yea, even all Nations, *verf.* 24. The Justice of *God*, in punishing National breach of Covenant, will be so mainifected, and magnified, that all Men may know, and must acknowledge it. Not only the Godly will be affected with horror, and rivers of Tears will run down their eyes, and they will wish their heads were fountains of Tears, at the fight of the fin procuring, and the judgement punishing: Nor only faithful *Teachers,*that warned the people of these things before, will observe when they come to pass. *Jer.* 5. 19. To whom the mouth of the Lord hath spoken, that they may declare, for what the Land perisheth, who can easily tell, that it is for forsaking the Lord, and His Covenant, *Jer.* 9. 12, 13 *Jer.* 16. 10, 11. Nor Covenant breakers themselves, that are left in that day, when many evils and troubles befall them, will say, *are not these evils come upon us, because our God is not among us?* Deut. 31. 17. And will be forced to acknowledge that the Lord is righteous, 2 *Chron.* 12. 5, 6. But it shall be obferved and acknowledged by the Generation to come, and by Strangers, and all Nations about, 2 *Chron.* 7. 19 &c. *Jer.* 22. 8, 9. Yea by Adverfaries, imployed as the Instruments of these punishments, *Lev* 26. 32, *I will bring the Land to defolation, and your enemies which dwell therein, shall be astonished at it.* Jer. 40 2, *Nebuzaradan,*the chief Captain of the Guard, faid to the Prophet, *The Lord thy God bath pronounced this evil upon this place, now the Lord hath brought it, and done according as He hath faid, because ye have finned against the Lord, and have not obeyed his voice, therefore this thing is come upon you.* Jer. 50. 7, *All that found them have devoured them, and their Adverfaries faid, we offend not, because they have finned against the Lord the habitation of juftice, even the Lord, the hope of their fathers.*

It may be a Queftion, *Why is the punishment of National breach* *Queft.* 17 *of Covenant fo publick, that it is obferved of Pofterity, and Strangers ?* *Anf:* 1. To vindicate the glory of God, which would be very much obfcured and wronged, in the fight of the Nations, if the punishment were not as publick as the fin, which was obferved by them; And to vindicate true Religion, from the imputation of allowing perjury, hateful to all Nations. 2. To proportion the punishment with the fin, in Juftice, *Jer:* 5: 19: Ezek: 16: 59: the defpifing the Oath of *God*, and breaking His Covenant was publict and National, and therefore muft be punished with

with Judgements, that are publick and National. 3. To remove the ftumbling-block from the Nations about, and Pofterity, that this im. punity would lay before them, if fuch a fin might pafs without fignal and ftupendious ftrokes. And to fet up a Beacon, to warn all of the hazard of fplitting upon this Rock. And as the warning of it is a witnefs againft them that will do the like, *Deut:* 31: 21: So, much more the accomplifhment will be. All Nations have obferved and admired *Scotlands* Eminency, when owning *Gods Covenant*: All Nations have again defpifed, derided, and hiffed at our unparalleled *perjury*, that the very *Turks* blufh to hear of. It may be, if Repentance prevent it not, as we have been a hiffing and a taunting proverb, for the guilt of it, fo we may be a curfe and execration, for the punifhment of it.

2. The thing they fhall obferve, or the occafion of their obferving, is (1) *When they fee the plagues of the Land, and the ficknefles which the Lord hath laid upon it;* ver: 22: Land plagues are here threatned, for this *Land-fin* of breach of Covenant; And Land-ficknefles of all forts, Moral and Phyfical, even all mentioned *Lev.* 26. and *Deut.* 28. The plague of the Sword, of Tyrannizing Rulers or inwading Enemies, or opprefling Robbers or Rebells, the plague of Famine, Dearth or Poverty, the plague of Peftilence, or infecting contagious Difeafles and Sicknefles on Peoples Carcafes or Spirits, or on the managements and Adminiftrations of publick Interefts, making a Sick and Difturbed Church and State. Whence come all thefe Diftempers? Whence have flowed all thefe Grievances, under which *Scotland* hath groaned thefe 40 years? The beft grounded Anfwer is only this, *Becaufe we have forefaken the Covenant of the Lord God of our fathers.* We have feen many of thefe plagues and ficknefles already, we may fee yet more, if we live. 2. *And that the whole land there-* *Verfe 23.* *of is brimftone and falt, and burning, and that it is not fown, nor beareth, nor any grafs groweth therein, like the overthrow of Sodom and Gomorrhah, Admah, and Zeboim, which the Lord overthrew in his anger, and in His wrath;* ver: 23: Here is threatned (thô not peremptorly predicted as the reft is) the total and final defolation of the Land of Ifrael, if they fhould forfake the Covenant of the Lord God of their fathers, which is compared *ad terrorem*, or *ad equivalentiam*, to the overthrow of the Cities of the plain. The Lord doth not alwayes *ad literam* fulfill this threatning; but here fhews, what every Land, avowing and perfifting in breach of Covenant, may fear, and in Juftice expect. Juftice requires, that any land guilty of *Sodoms* fins, fhould be lyable to its Judgements. If we compare *Scotlands* fins, and breaches of Covenant, with the fins of thefe Cities, we fhal find

none of thefe abominations here wanting ; which brought down juſt vengeance on the Cities of the plain ; In *Gen: 19:chap:* We find their fins were chiefly the breaches of the *ſeventh Command.* And in *Ezek. 16. 49:* thefe were their Iniquities, *Pride, fulneſs of Bread, abundance of Idleneſs, neither did ſhe ſtrengthen the hand of the poor and needy, and they were haughty, and committed abomination, therefore the Lord took them away as He ſaw good.* In no Nation under Heaven thefe fins have a louder Cry for Vengeance, than in *Scotland,* which declares thefe fins and many more that *Sodom* was never in capacity to commit, without ſhame or fear as *Sodom,* and hides them not, *Iſa. 3. 9.* Whoſe Rulers, of a long time, have been *Rulers of Sodom,* and whoſe people have been *People of Gomorrah,* Iſa. 1. 10. Yea, we are lyable to the Lords Upbraidings more than *Sodom,* Math. 11.23. 24. For if the mighty works which have been done in *Scotland,* had been done in *Sodom,* it would have remained untill this day , therefore it may be feared it ſhall be more tollerable for the land of *Sodom ,* in the day of judgement, then for *Scotland.* And from what of this threatned curfe of the Covenant we have feen accompliſhed in any meafure, we may have grouud to fear what further ſhall be feen in future fulfilments of it, if repentance do not prevent it. We have feen parts of the Land, fometime fruitful, and well inhabited, and many Families formerly well provided, in our day laid defolate, neither fown nor reaped: We have feen fome Cities almoſt burnt to aſhes, we have feen great Poverty and Sterility in the Land. What is the Caufe? Even this, *becauſe we have forſaken the Covenaut of the Lord God of our fathers.* Iſa. 24. 5, 6. *The earth hath been defiled under the inhabitants thereof, breauſe they have tranſgreſſed the Laws, changed the Ordinance, broken the everlaſting Covenant, therefore hath the Curſe devoured the earth.*

From all this here threatned as the confequent puniſhment Queſt. 18. of National breach of Covenant, we may further inquire, *What may this Nation, or any other guilty of the like Perjury, fear or expect in juſtice, in the day He viſits us?* Befides the *Text,* we may gather, *in cumulo,* thefe *Curſes* of the Covenant. [1] Terrors and tormenting panick diſtracting Fears, the hag of guilty Confciences, Lev. 26. 16. Caufing to flee when none purfues, *v.* 17. 36. Deut. 28. 67. Felt in part already, in many ſhameful yeeldings, flights, and difcomfiturs [2] Mortal & contagious diſtempers of body, confumptions, burning agues, Levit. 26. 16. Peſtilence *v.* 25 Inflammations, Deut. 23. 21; 22. Plagues, *v.* 27, 35, 59, 61. The great mortality now very ordinary in the Land, is the fruit of breach of Covenant. [3] Enemies Depradations, Depopulations and Devaſtations, eating up the feed, Lev. 26. 16. Slaying and chaſing, *v.* 17. A Sword to avenge

the

the quarrel of the Covenant, r 25. Deut. 28. 25, 3
15. Jer. 15. 2. Jer. 34. 18, 20. Who can tell but th
in Brittain and Ireland, may avenge the quarrel of H
[4] Tyrants domination, Levit. 26. 17. Deut. 28. 4
preſſion under the two preceeding Tyrants;hath been
ment of our breach of Covenant: [5] Barrenneſs
the ground, Levit. 26. 19, 20. Deut. 28. 23, 24. Iſa. 2
devouring, Lev. 26. 22. Ier. 15. 3: The Lord car
men as bad as beaſts. [7] Famine, Levit. 26: 26, 20
Ier. 15. 2. Many poor people have felt ſomewhat o
the Lord to reach the rich alſo when he will. [8] De
Sanctuaries, Lev. 26. 31, 32, 34. 2. King. 17. 15.
have long languiſhed under Sanctuary deſolations
low. [9] Exile and ſlavery, Lev. 26: 33, 38: Deut: 2
This hath been in part literally accompliſhed , i
many to America;more may be coming. [10] A co
and upon all enjoyments and employments, Deut.
24: 20: Since ever we forſook the Lord, nothing ha
[11] Infatuation, Deut: 28: 28: Quos Deos vult perde
written on all our projects, for which we are a ſcor
Nations about us. [12] Deſertion from God, and
Deut: 31: 17: Jer: 15: 1: Viſibly ſeen in Ordinances
fruit of our forſaking His Covenant. In a word,
31: 17: All evills, even to utter deſtruction, Joſh
which, our hearts may meditate Terror.

3. Their Enquiry or Queſtion, upon
Verſ. 24. the tremendous puniſhment of this ſin,
Queſt. 19: Lord done this unto this Land? What meanet
anger? This is frequently predicted to be th
rors, that ſhall obſerve the National Puniſhment
ſins: As in the caſe of the Temples deſolation for 7
1 Kings 9. 8, 9. 2 Chron. 7. 21, 22. The like alſo,
this ſhall be the queſtion of the Nations, it will be e
is not ſo at the beginning of the Lords contendings.
queſtion of the Apoſtatizing Generation it ſelf; T
Watch-men, inſtructed of God, will anſwer it ſuit
16. 10. It is not eaſie to find the wiſe man that may
whom the mouth of the Lord hath ſpoken, that he may decl
periſheth, Jer. 9. 12, 13. The moſt guilty may al

of the Lands trouble,as *Ahab* faid to *Elijab*,1 *King*.18.
Prophets not difcovering the Lands iniquity,may *fee*
r *of banifbment*, Lam. 2. 14. However,it will be no mif-
veral caufes of wrath againft *Scotland*,even any,or all
:wn Vengeance upon any Ger eration of wrath recor-
or in any Hiftory;fuch as,*Profanity* of all forts,*Hypocri-*
reacbery,*Pride*,*Blood* and *Oppreffion*,*Contempt of the Gofpel*
:d with the greateft aggravations. With thefe indeed
troubled,polluted,and for the fame is yet perifhing :
nich hath incenfed the anger of the Lord to all this
nd remains to be, *Breach of Covenant*. And all thefe
imply becaufe Breaches of the Law of *God*,but as un-
avation, that they have been, and are Breaches of
ident from,
nfwer here given, *Becaufe they have forfaken* Verf. 25.
ird *God of their fathers,* *which he made with*
them forth out of the Land of, *Egypt*, ver. 25. This An-
d from *Men*, all Men, that are Men of any confide-
5. 19.[.]*Jer*. 9. 13. *Jer*. 16. 10. *Covenant-breakers* them-
Strangers, 2 Chron. 7. 21, 22. *Jer*. 22. 8, 9. Let it
wherefore hath the Lord done thus unto *Scotland* ?
heat of all this great anger, in which it hath been
e 40 years,and yet not confumed? The *Anfwer* muft
n the Covenant *&c*. It appears hence,that breach of
fin, and caufe of wrath. And is further confirmed
ings of wrath for it, Levit. 26, 25. *Deut*. 31. 16, 17.
bron. 7. 21,22. *Jer*. 22. 8, 9. From fad and ftupen-
iefe Threatnings, *Jofh*. 7. 11, 15. 2 *Kings* 17. 15. *&c*.
rom the confeffions and complaints of it, 1 *King*: 19,
It may be alfo obferved from hence, that no fin is
an breach of Covenant, as appears from thefe words,
this *Anfwer* of the Nations. 1. Aggravates this fin in
iecifies the particular kind of it, *v*: 26. 3. Juftifies
:, *v*. 27, 28.
ted the heinoufnefs of breach of Covenant, in a con-
: fhews forth its hatefulnefs.There are feveral degrees
the worft.
How may a Nation be guilty of breach of Covenant ? *Anf*:
ly (1) by tranfgreffing any of the Articles of it, as
er gods, *ver*: 26 ; putting forth the hand to any ac-

curfed

ourſed thing, which, thô it was the perſonal ſin of a
whole Congregation was involved in it, *Joſh: 7: 11,*
it is diſcovered, and yet connived at, not witneſſed aga
over. But (2) by raſhneſs or falſhood in making it,
falſly in making a Covenant, when it is not taken in truth
judgement, when only in Hypocritical flatterie, with
faſt hearts it is engaged into, *Pſal: 78. 36, 37.* (3) By
4: 23: *Take heed unto your ſelves leſt ye forget the Covenant*
Forgetting is a ſtep towards forſaking. *Pſal: 44: 17:*
venant ſhould not be forgotten, *Jer: 50: 5.* (4) By
lude it, and Arguments to defend the breach of it, F
deſpiſing and undervaluing the Bond of it, *Ezek: 16:*
(6) By defection to the iniquities abjured in it, *Jerem*
changing the inſtitutions ſworn to be maintained, 1
the State Government, without conſulting *Divine dire*
Hoſ: 8: 1, 4. Or the Church. Government, without r
of the revealed will of Chriſt, *2 Chron. 13. 9, 10, 11.*
it, and downright denying the obligation of it, *Da*
ſtating an oppoſition to it, and perſecuting them that
19. 10. Dan. 11. 30. The two laſt are properly *forſa*
which is more then breaking it, (here n
Queſt. 21. anſwer to this *Queſt. What are the Aggra*
      This *Forſaking,* implying willing and
reſolution, and preſumption in avowing the breach c
length in perjury, yet ſhort of the amount of *Scotlan*
ſrontery in enacting the breach of it, making the ren
lification of perſons capable of publick Truſt, **burn**
of the Hangman, and making the owning of it Cri
is a *forſaking* of the Covenant, which, as it includes a
mandments of God, which hath a brand of a hateful he
18: *2 Chron: 12: 1, 5: Ezra 9: 10: Jer: 9: 13.* So, it i
greater aggravation, to forſake a Covenant of ſo lon
tual Covenant, *Jer: 50: 5.* A Covenant ſo holy, *Dan:*
ſo ſolemnly engaged into , *Jer: 34: 18:* ſo frequently
ſuch ſanctions, certificacions, adjurations and curſes,
and *Jer: 11: 2, 3.* Further, it is a forſaking of the
God. Tho it were but a mans Covenant, yet it cc
without the baſeſt of treacherie, much more to forſ
which is to forſake Himſelf, a dreadful ſin, ſo
Scripture, *Deut. 31. 16. Deut. 32. 15. Joſh. 24. 1*

:rs from Slavery, whofe mercy and faithfulnefs their
ced, and from their experience of the good of keep-
Iim, had commended it to their pofterity; A Co-
:e date, or a new invention, but tranfmitted from
renant, which,upon that head, the Lord hath refpeft
1, fometimes He will not deftroy, but have com-
orthy pofterity, 2 *King.* 13: 23. This is charged as
of breaking Covenant, *Jer.* 11. 10. *Mal.* 2. 10. Be-
:nant of their Fathers, or of the God of their Fathers.
I the particular way of their forfaking the
r they went and ferved other gods, and wor- *Verf.* 26:
this is the groffeft way of breaking Covenant, to
her Gods: But this hath alfo its degrees, whether
ifidered as a breach of the Firft, or of the Second
was fhewed before, and undeniable in the Scriptures.
d internal Idolatry. There is Idolatry that hath a
dolatry alfo that may pretend the true objeft of wor-
in a worfhip not of His appointment. However,
e noted, that *Service* and *Worfhip* is all one. Hence
ı of *Dowleia* and *Latreia* is groundlefs and Anti-fcrip-
or *Worfhiping* of other gods, is aggravated from two
' were *gods whom they knew not,* worfhiping *an unknown*
c *Motto* of the *Athenian* Alter) is a peculiar ftretch of
ition, *Act.* 17: 22, 23: Ignorance then (of the objeft,
rfhip) is not the *Mother* but the *Murther* of true De-
luction of any unknown or uncouth thing, whether
ır manner of worfhip, or any New Invention, or
rvice or worfhip of God, is hence inferred to be a
. [2] They were gods *whom he had not given unto*
then be received, admitted, or allowed in worfhip
which God hath not given, granted, or command-
His Law and Covenant. His Law is fo perfect, that

not only what He hath *forbidden* is fin, but what He hath not *commanded* in Religious fervice.

3. Here is juftified the punifhment of that forfaking of the *Verf.* 27,28: Lords Covenant, *ver:* 27, 28: (1) In vindicating the juftice of it, in that all the effect of the *Anger of the Lord kindled againft the Land, v: 27:* was according to the *Curfes that are written in this book.* The punifhment of a Land breaking Covenant, is only what it deferves, and what the Lord hath threatned in the Scriptures. (2) In indicating and acknowledging the feverity of it, *v. 28.* How *the Lord rooted them out of their Land in anger, and in wrath, and in great indignation &c.* Hence it may be inferred, that if Covenanters will not *extirpate* what pollutes the Land, according to their Engagements, the Lord will be provoked to extirpate them out of the Land, according to His Word.

VI. In the clofe, *verf.* ult. there is a *Conclufory* Corollary fub-*Verf.* 29. joined to all. *The fecret things belong unto the Liad our God: but thofe things which are revealed belong unto us, and to our Children for ever, that we may do all the words of this Law.* This may be taken either abftractly, as an Apothegm by it felf, or with relation to what follows in the next *chapter,* or to what preceeds in *this.* Sin and Duty is here clearly revealed, and that fhould be the matter of our exercife: But Events are fecrets belonging to the Lord. He hath revealed it is our duty to *keep the words of this Covenant and do them:* But, who fhall endure to the end fo doing, is a fecret known to Himfelf. He hath revealed it is our duty to *enter into Covenant with the Lord our God, that He may eftablifh us for a people unto Himfelf:* But who fhall get this priviledge made good unto them, without reverfion: Or, who fhall *turn away,* and have a *root that beareth Gall and Wormwood,* &c. is a fecret. In the general it is revealed that the keepers of the Covenant fhall have the bleffings of it fecured, and the breakers fhall have the curfes ratified: But who they fhall be by name and furname, is a fecret belonging unto the Lord. He hath clearly revealed, that the great procuring caufe of Divine Vengeance, is, *Forfaking the Covenant:* But *when* He will inflict and execute this Vengeance, *how,* and *upon* whom, and *by* whom or *what* Inftruments, or in what *meafure,* or how *long,* Thefe are fecrets. Again, in the following *Chap.* He hath clearly revealed when thefe Threatnings have come upon us, and we fhall call them to mind, even in captivity, and fhall *return unto the Lord our God, and fhall obey His voice, that then the Lord our God will turn our Captivity, and will have Compaffion upon us.* &c. But as for the *feafons* of it, *it is not for us to know them,* Act. 1. 7. Whither it fhall be at this time, in our day, or afterwards;

these difpenfations or inftruments now made ufe of,
things belonging to the Lord our God.

e to this *Introduction*; it is apparent from what is faid
doubts, or dark difficulties about *National Covenants*,
lved from this *Chapter*, and feen to be, not among
lled with, but among the *Things Revealed*, belong-
ildren. Particularly thefe *Queftions* here touched,
mbling ftones to many, and Topicks of objections
Covenants, are in fome meafure cleared. Which
e prefented to the Readers view.

it be *Lawful* and *expedient* for Nations to enter into Cove-
verf. 1.
Nature of this Covenanting ? ibid.
ay be done without the Magiftrate ? Or, when it is fo,
nding ? ibid.
ovenant is *Renewed*, may it be done with Alterations and
time ? ibid.
e Motives *to Renew the Covenant* ? from v. 2: to v. 9.
keep *Covenant* ? from v. 9.
venant be renewed without the Primores, when they will
10:
ren be admitted to the Covenant ? from v: 11.
ts obliged, or may they be admitted to the Covenant ? ibid.
ovenant bind the abfent, and them that did not take it ?

Covenant be impofed upon all ? or may all be admitted to

loofe the obligation of it ? from v: 12.
better fhall we be of making and keeping a National Cove-

gation of National Covenants (upon the matter Law-
ding upon pofterity. from ver: 15.
he chief tentations *inducing to the fin of Covenant-break-
radual fteps of it ?* from 16: to 20.
: the Curfes and Punifhments *threatned againft Cove-
*, from v. 20.
he punifhment of *National breach of Covenant fo* Publick,
ferity and Strangers ? from ver. 22: &c.
he threatned Punifhment of National breach of Covenant ?
Q. 12.

Q. 19. *What is the procuring* Cause *of all the*Nations Miseries*?*from *v:* 24:25
Q. 20. *How may a* Nation *be* guilty *of breach of Covenant?* from *v:* 25:
Q. 21. *What are the* aggravations *of that sin?* ibid:

THese being premised, there is the less need to inlarge in the vindi
cation of the *Renovation* of these Covenants, here subjoyned, as they
were *Sworn* and *Subscribed* at *Lesmahego.* March, 3. 1689. Their *Motives*
are before touched on *Question* 4. from *verf.* 2. to 9. They Consider
ed what the Lord had done before their eyes, the great tentations in their
day, the signs and the great wonders of the Wisdom, Faithfulness, Power
Justice and Goodness of the Lord, appearing in His way with them and
their Fathers.They Considered the univerfal Obduration, Stupidity
and unanswerableness to these wonders in themselves and others, how
they had not gotten hearts to perceive,nor eyes to fee in to that very day
They Considered the Lords greacious Conduct of them and their fathers
and their own experience of His care and kindness towards them, in pro
viding fo tenderly and wonderfully all necessaries for their *Wildernefs* Lo
They considered, how at length the Lord helped them to overcome two
Kings,that eudeavoured by all means to destroy them. They confide
red, that, as the Lord promises prosperity to the keeping, and doing
the words of His Covenant; So, in the dayes of their Fathers, when
they entered into, and kept Covenant with God, He prospered them
in all that they undertook, went forth with their Armies, and made
their Enemies to fall down before them, testifying in His providence
His approbation of His peoples Covenanting. They considered also
how these Covenants (thô of Eternal obligation, as is cleared *Queft.* 14
from *verf.* 15.) were broken, their breaches enacted by Law, *they were*
Burnt, the owning of them declared Criminal by an Act of *Queensberrie.*
Parliament, and the obligation of them,was like to be totally buried in
oblivion. And therefore,as they thought this a *Cafe of Confeffion,*when they
could do no more,to give their Teftimony for the Covenants, with pro
feffion of the Sorrow of their hearts, and abhorrence of their fouls a
gainst these indignities (as was done in the Printed *Teftimony, anno.* 1688.
So, upon the fame motives, they thought it no lefs neceffary, now, in
this oppurtunity, to revive the memory of them, and at leaft to break
the ice for others to renew them more Solemnly. At that Critical fea
fon, especially, when in the univerfal expectation of War, upon the
change of the Government,all parties were Affociating for their own de
fence, and afferting the quarrell and party they would efpoufe: They
alfo thought it expedient, by the renewing of these ancient Covenants

ley would avouch, and appear for; what King
nd upon what termes they would offer, and oblige
e prefent Government, then to be eftablifhed, who
revolt from the former, and for this end, to make
Affociation.

a great deal of clamour by many, that this was an
ous Action, without all Authority, or concurrence
uthority to tender an Oath. But as this is loofed
, on *Queft*. 3, and *Q*.7. from *v.* 1. and *v.* 10. So we
ntering into, and renewing Covenants, for Defence
ty, without the Authority then regnant, in feveral
fince the eftablifhed Reformation; As that Covenant
7, for the maintenance and advancement of Re-
ace of one another adhering to it. Another Cove-
And at *Stirling*, the fame year. Another at *Leith*,
t *Air*, 1552. All thefe without the concurrence of
And in the year 1638, the National Covenant was
obtained Authority for it. And *anno* 1666. at *Lanerk*,
nneft and faithful patriots renewed the Solemn
and againft the Authority that was then. But this
vas without Authority, yet it was not againft Au-
time of the *Interregnum*, before the fettlement of
ufe, in ftead of the ufual Expreffions of *the King*, & *his*
the margent, *His Highnefs*, or *the Civil Magiftrate*, be-
as not then declared. And that party who renewed
not pretend to any Authority to do it as a *National*
Nation; Only to take on the vowes of God upon
vite others to do the like. If thofe that tendered
ime, did take upon them any Authority, it was
any, but rather to exclude fome from it, and to
to it, who were grofsly ignorant and fcandalous,
them the hazard of fwearing falfely. And dif-
e name of the Lord, to devour thefe holy things.
ace to fome and occafion of obloquie againft the
fi d above, by what is faid on *Queft*. 11. from *v.*
d by an Act of Affembly, *July* 20. *Sff*. 12. *anno*
ofs Complyers from the Covenant, and Ordaining
who were debarred, fhould be admitted, but fuch
fh uld be found for fome Competent time, before
heir Repentance , to have in their ordinary Con-

E   " verfa-

"verfations given Teftimony of their diflike of thefe
it is not to be forgotten, when the Minifter was enla
fuch as had voluntarly given in the fame to him, w
Write, before hand ·(*viz.* fome that had gone a g
and Scandalous exceffes, with that Impoftor *John Gil*
who had been involved in feveral fad defeétions, in th
as, Hearing the *Curats*, paying the *Cefs*, taking th
&c.) Offering, and defiring to make publick Ack
the Congregation (then in the *Fields*)of thefe thei
only feveral others, who had not given up their r
openly declared that they were guilty of feveral fl
alfo fome declared their guilt of perfonal *Scandals*,
nifter was neceffitate feveral times to crave forbeara
far fpent, that (after the Covenants were fworn) th
was hereby (happily) prevented untill night, w
*Church.*The great out cry is againft the Alterations
Renovation of the Covenants : But as this objeétion
is faid above on *Quest.* 4. from *verfe* 1. So, that R
tional Covenant, in the year 1638, With very la
modate to the time,is a precedent juftifying any Alt
in the Covenants Renewed at *Lefmahego* , which at
of the Covenants, that cannot fuit the prefent time
every Alteration, marked·only in the Margent, w
old words.

There are indeed many Additions in the *Ackn*
Engagement to duties (which alfo were then Solemn
thefe Late unhappy times of defeétion have produ
than could be Confeffed· in that Acknowle
But the whole of the former is retained in a L
the Additions fubjoyned in a *Leffer Charaéter* , fc
fame is done, upon the fame grounds , in the Er
annexed. In the *former* , the fins of the time are a
tially, without concealing any of their own, fo far
more than the fins of any other party. In the L
Covenant are particularly and plainly engaged in
Confcience of them, even thofe that are, or hav
That if others may not hereby be excited to confi
felves might come to, and intertain a determined (
halt between two opinions. And to the end the M
ligation of the Covenants may be confidered an

)f are antecedently Commanded, and the fins there-
dden, thô there had been no fuperadded Covenant;
knowledgment of fins (according to the Order of
ovenant, which are there repeated) the Scriptures
ticle and Claufe thereof, are annexed.

7ion which is moft commonly infifted on, and feems
is, That thô it were tolerable to Renew the National
a party in Scotland to renew the Solemn League and Co-
is folly and prefumption,without their concurrence
ue without Colleagues being abfurd and ridiculous.
re a very thorny point, if it were pleaded or pre-
n League and Covenant was, or is to be Renewed, ei-
he whole body of Scotland, in the prefent circum-
ame and adequate formality, confideration, and
and Confederation with England or Ireland, as it was
   that is , as a League Offenfive and Defenfive
:ody of thefe Kingdoms, and the Noblemen, Ba-
:lemen, Citizens, Burgeffes, Minifters of the Gof-
of all forts, in Scotland, England and Ireland; For
1an Affociation with the Prelatical and Malignant
which, as the cafe now ftands, it were very hard to
for Religion, between thefe Nations, albeit their
:nt were obtained,for fear of a finful Affociation, fo
1 Scripture, except they were more Reformed, and
:formation, and except the things to be Reformed
>articularly expreffed, with accommodation to the
: thefe times; that were not known, and could not
t making of the Solemn League and Covenant : But it
: whole Nation, or even a party in it, renew That
s it is a Covenant with God: wherein He is refpected
>ut Party Contracting, or with whom they Contract,
w obedience: Wherein alfo, they oblige themfelves
th reference to God or Man, or thofe that fome-
now broken off from the League, but what they are
y , if there had never been any fuch Covenant, or
   And if it be Confidered as a League or Affociati-
not in the fame extent as formerly, but only with
enew it, or with all that owne it in Scotland, England
is Confideration, thefe words in the begining of the

Solemn League and *Covenant*, expreſſing the ſeveral ranks, and the extent of the Covenanters were not read, at the Renewing of it at *Leſmahego*. Becauſe they owned themſelves to be under a League with none, bnt ſuch as owned the Covenanted Reformation. Nor is it altogether unprecedented, that a Nation Renewing the Covenant, from which their Colleagues have receded. The Renovation of it in *Scotland*, anno 1649, was, after the prevailing power of *England* did reſile from their Engagements ; thô ſome did then, as to this day a few do adhere to them. All the Tribes of *Iſrael* were once in Covenant together: The revolt of the Ten Tribes, did not hinder the Godly in *Judab* to renew it, in the dayes of *Aſa*, *Hezekiah*, *Joſiab*, nor did it preclude a ſmal party of *Ephraim Manaſſeb*, &c. to take part in it, 2 *Chron* 15. 9, 12. But thô there might be ſome informality or inconveniency in keeping the old Form of the *Solemn League*, with ſuch alterations only annoted on the *Margent*, as might make it accommodable to the preſent time: And perhaps it had been more ſuitable, to frame it altogether in a New Form, if the Repreſentatives of Church and State had conceitred : Yet, that party at *Leſmahego*, not daring to take ſo much upon them, and therefore adhering to both Matter and Form, ſo far as it could ſerve the time, and the Engagements thereof quadrate with their capacities, are not to be raſh'y condemned for their Renewing old Vows, which were (and in ſo far only as they were) before, and then, and are alwayes binding. Yea rather it were ſuitable and ſeaſonable for the Repreſentatives (who can eaſily mend, what was not within their (pherelto do) in ſtead of deſpiſing the meannſs of that party, and carping at the imperfections of that action, to imitate their Zeal, in Renewing theſe National Engagements, with ſolemn Acknowlegements of the Breaches thereof, in a Form that will better pleaſe them. This would be a notable mean of turning away the Lords fierce Wrath from the Nation, 2 *Chron.* 29. 10. Hereby Reformation in Church and State might be promoted and preſerved ; Order and Union in the Church, which hath been long wanting, might be ſettled and eſtabliſhed; Former Defections might be honeſtly and honourably removed and remedied; Future Innovations and Corruptions, Schiſmes and D'ſorders might be prevented and precluded; And all Malignant Enemies of Reformation might be by this Teſt diſcovered, and excluded from all Truſt in Church or State, and capacity to do either hurt : Yet without any conſtraint or reſtrain' upon any Mans true liberty. How pleaſant and acceptable, both to God and Man, would it be, as it may be hoped it will be, when the Lords people in theſe Lands, now ſore and long ſcattered and divided, ſhall return going and weeping, ſeeking the Lord their God, and asking the way to *Zion* with their Faces thitherward, That, at leaſt the Owners & Lovers of Reformation, were ſaying, Come and let us joyn our ſelves unto the Lord, in a perpetual *Covenant*, that ſhall not be forgotten.

THE

THE

NATIONAL COVENANT

O R,

The Confeſſion of Faith *of the Kirk of* Scotland, *ſubſcribed at firſt by the Kings Majeſty and his Houſhold, in the year* 1580. *Thereafter, by Perſons of all ranks, in the year* 1581. *By Ordinance of the Lords of the Secret Council, and Acts of the* General Aſſembly. *Subſcribed again by all ſorts of Perſons in the year* 1590. *By a new Ordinance of Council, at the deſire of the* General Aſſembly: *With a general Band for maintainance of the true Religion and the Kings Perſon. And ſubſcribed in the year* 1638. *By the Noblemen, Barons, Gentlemen, Burgeſſes, Miniſters, and Commons, then underſubſcribing. Together, with their reſolution and promiſes for the cauſes after ſpecified, To maintain the ſaid true Religion, and the Kings Majeſty, according to the* Confeſſion foreſaid, *and Act of Parliament. And thereafter, upon the Supplication of the General Aſſembly to* His Majeſties *high Commiſſioner and the Lords of his Majeſties Honourable Privy Council, ſubſcribed again in the Year* 1639. *by Ordinance of Council, and Act of General Aſſembly. And now again by Us this preſent Year* 1689. *Acknowledging the publick breaches thereof, and engaging to the Duties contained therein, with Accommodation to our Caſe and Time.*

WE All, and every one of Us underwritten, Proteſt, that, after long and due Examination of our own Conſciences, in matters of true and falſe Religion. We are now throughly reſolved of the Truth, by the Word and Spirit of God; and therefore we believe with our hearts, confeſs with our mouths, ſubſcribe with our hands and onſtantly affirm before God, and the whole World, that this only is he true Chriſtian Faith and Religion, pleaſing God, and bringing Salvation to Man, which now is by the Mercy of God reyealed to the world,

by

by the preaching of the Bleſſed Evangel, and re
defended by many and ſundry notable
*and ſome- chiefly by the *Kirk of Scotland*, * *the Kin*
times by ſtates of this Realme, as Gods eternal Tru
our Salvation: As more particularly is expreſſed i
Faith,ſtabliſhed,and publickly confirmed by ſund
and now of a long time hath been openly profeſ
jeſty , and whole body of this Realm, both in
the which Confeſſion and Form of Religion , 1
our Conſciences in all points, as unto Gods undo
ty, grounded only upon his written Word. An
and deteſt all contrary Religion and Doctrine : 1
Papiſtry,in general and particular heads, even as
and confuted by the *Word of God*, and *Kirk of Scotla*
deteſt and refuſe the uſurped Authority of that R
the Scriptures of God, upon the Kirk, the Civil
ſcience of Men, all his Tyrannous Laws made t
againſt our Chriſtian Liberty, his erroneous Doc
ency of the written Word, the perfection of th
Chriſt, and His bleſſed Evangel. His corruptec
Original Sin, our natural Inability and Rebell
Juſtification by Faith only, our imperfect Sanctiſ
to the Law,the Nature,Number, and Uſe of the
five baſtard Sacraments, with all his Rites,Ceren
rine added to the miniſtration of the true Sacramo
of God. His cruel judgement againſt Infants de
crament: His abſolute neceſſity of Baptiſm, his b
Tranſubſtantiation, or Real preſence of Chriſt's
and receiving of the ſame by the wicked, or Boc
penſations with ſolemn Oaths,Perjuries,and degre
den in the Word: his cruelty againſt the Innocer
liſh Maſs: his blaſphemous 'Prieſt-hood , profa
of the Dead and the Quick,his Canonization of
gels or Saints departed, worſhipping of Imagery,
dedicating of Kirks, Altars,Dayes, Vowes to Cre
Prayers for the Dead, praying or ſpeaking in a ſ
his Proceſſions, and blaſphemous Litany,and mu
Mediators: his manifold Orders,auricular Confe
uncertain Repentance; his general and doubtſom

Men for their fins, his Juſtification by Works, *opus operatum*, Works Supererogation, Merits, Pardons, Peregrinations, and Stations: his ſly Water, baptiſing of Bells, conjuring of Spirits, Croſſing, Saning, ſointing, Conjuring, hallawing of Gods good Creatures, with the ſuſtitious opinion joyned therewith: his worldly Monarchy, and wicked erarchy: his three ſolemn Vowes, with all his Shavellings of ſundry ſorts : Erroneous & Bloody Decrees made at *Trent*, with all the Subſcribers d Approvers of that cruel & bloody Band, conjured againſt the Kirk God: And Finally, we deteſt all his vain Allegories, Rites, Signes and ſaditions, brought into the Kirk, without or againſt the Word of God, d Doctrine of this true reformed Kirk, to the which we joyn our ſelves llingly, in Doctrine, Faith, Religion, Diſcipline , and uſe of the ſly Sacraments, as lively Members of the ſame, in Chriſt our Head : omiſing and Swearing by the *Great Name of the Lord our God*, that we ill continue in the obedience of the Doctrine and Diſcipline of this rk, and ſhall defend the ſame according to our Vocation and Power, the dayes of our lives, under the pains contained in the Law, and nger both of Body and Soul, in the day of Gods fearful Judgement ; ſd ſeing that many are ſtirred up by Satan, and that Roman Antiriſt, to promiſe, ſwear, ſubſcribe, and for a time uſe the Holy Sacraents in the Kirk deceitfully againſt their own Conſciences, minding erehy, firſt under the external Cloak of Religion, to corrupt and ſubſrt ſecretly Gods true Religion within the Kirk, and afterward, when ne may ſerve, to become open Enemies, and Perſecutors of the ſame ſder vain hope of the Popes Diſpenſation, deviſed againſt the Word God, to his greater conluſion , and their double condemnation in the y of the Lord Jeſus.

We, therefore, willing to take away all ſuſpicion of Hypocriſie, and ſuch double dealing with God and His Kirk, Proteſt, and call *The archer of all hearts* for witneſs, that our minds and hearts, do fully ſree with this Our *Confeſſion*, *Promiſe*, *Oath*, and *Subſcription*, ſo that We e not moved for any worldly reſpect, but are perſwaded only in Our ſnſciences, through the knowledge and love of Gods true Religion, ſinted in Our Hearts by the Holy Spirit, as we ſhall anſwer to Him the day, when the ſecrets of all hearts ſhall be diſcloſed. And becauſe ſ perceive that the quietneſs and ſtability of our Religion and Kirk, ſth depend upon the ſafety and good behaviour of * the ings Majeſty, as upon a comfortable Inſtrument of Gods ſercy, granted to this Country, for the maintaining of

* The lawfully eſtabliſhed Supreme Magiſtrat.

this

this Kirk, and miniftration of Juftice amongft us , we proteft and promife with our Hearts under the fame Oath, Hand writ, and Pains, that
we fhall defend his Perfon and Authority , with our goods, bodies and,
lives, in the defence of Chrift his Evangel , Liberties of our Countrey ,
miniftration of Juftice, and punifhment of Iniquity, againft all Enemies
within this Realm, or without, as we defire our God to be a ftrong and
merciful Defender to us in the day of our death, and coming of our
Lord Jefus Chrift: To whom with the Father, and the Holy Spirit, be
all Honour and Glory Eternally.

Like as many Acts of Parliament not only in general do abrogate, an-
nul, and refcind all Laws, Statutes, Acts, Conftitutions, Canons, civil
or municipal, with all other Ordinances and practick Penalties whatfoever, made in prejudice of the true Religion and Profeffors thereof;
Or, of the true Kirk difcipline, Jurisdiction, and Freedom thereof; Or
in favours of Idolatry and Superftition; Or of the Papiftical Kirk: As.
Act. 3. *Act.* 13. *Parl.* 1. *Act.* 23. *Parl.* 11. *Act* 114 *Parl.* 12 of King
James the fixth. That Pap.ftry and Superftition may be utterly fuppref-
fed according to the intention of the Acts of Parliament repeated in the
5. *Act. Parl.* 20. King *James* 6th. And to that end they ordain all Priefts
to be punifhed by manifold Civil and Ecclefiaftical pains, as Adverfaries
to Gods true Religiou preached, and by Law eftablifhed within this
Realm, *Act* 24. *Parl.* 11. King *James* 6th. As common Enemies to all
Chriftian Government, *Act* 18. *Parl.* 16. King *James* 6th. As Rebellers
and Gain-ftanders of our Soveraign Lords Authority, *Act* 47. *Parl.* 3. K.
James 6. And as Idolaters. *Act* 104. *Parl.* 7. King *James* 6. But alfo in
particular (by and attour the Confeffion of Faith) do abolifh and condemn the Popes Authority and Jurisdiction out of this Land, and orders
the Maintainers thereof to be punifhed, *Act* 2. *Parl.* 1. *Act* 51. *Parl.* 3 *Act.*
106. *Parl.* 7. *Act* 114. *Parl.* 12. King *James* 6. Do condemn the Popes
erroneous Doctrine repugnant to any of the Articles of the true and Chriftian Religion publickly preached, and by Law eftablifhed in this Realm:
And ordains the fpreaders and makers of Books or Libels, or Letters, or
Writs of that nature, to be punifhed, *Act* 46. *Parl.* 3. *Act* 106. *Parl.* 7.
Act 24. *Parl.* 11. King *James* 6. Do condemn all Baptifm conform to the
Popes Kirk, and the Idolatry of the Mafs, and ordains all Sayers, wil-
ful hearers, and concealers of the Mafs, the mantainers and refetters of
Priefts, Jefuits, traffiquing Papifts, to be punifhed without any excepti n
or reftriction, *Act* 5. *Parl.* 1. *Act* 120. *Parl.* 12. *Act* 164. *Parl.* 13. *Act* 193.
Parl. 14. *Act* 1. *Parl.* 19. *Act* 5. *Parl.* 20. K. *James* 6. Do condemn all er-
roneous

(41)

'rites,containing erroneous Dectrine. against the Re-
-fled, or maintaining superstitious Rites and Cere-
whereby the People are greatly abused , and or-
:gers of them to be punished, *Act* 25: *Parl:* 11: K. *James*
monuments and dregs of by-gone Idolatry, as go-
blerving the Festival dayes of the Saints, and such
id Papistical Rites , to the dishonour of God, can-
n, and fostering of great errour among the People,
of them to be punished for the second fault, as Ido-
7: K: *James* 6.

s of Parliament are conceaved for maintenance of
tian Religion, and the purity thereof in Doctrine
e true Church of God', the liberty and freedom
ional, Synodal Assemblies, Presbyteries, Sessions,
id Jurisdiction thereof, as that purity of Religion
iurch was uled, professed, exercised, preached and
o the Reformation of Religion in this Realm. As
;: *Act Parl:* 7: *Act* 23: *Parl* 11: *Act* 114: *Parl:* 12: *Act*
g *James* 6. Ratified by the 4 *Act* of King *Charles* I.
'l. I. and 68 *Act Parl.* 6. of K. *James* 6. in the year
:es the Ministers of the blessed Evangel, whom God
iifed up, or hereafter should raise, agreeing with
i in Doctrine, and Administration of the Sacra-
ple that professed Christ, as He was then offered in
th communicate with the Holy Sacraments, (as in
if this Realm they were publickly administrat) ac-
ssion of Faith, to be the True and Holy Kirk of
is Realm, and decerns and declares all and sundry,
the Word of the Evangel, received and approved,
'onfession of Faith, professed in Parliament, in the
ipecified also in the first Parliament of K. *James* 6.
irefent Parliament, more particularly do specifie ;
ininistration of the Holy Sacraments, as they were
be no Members of the said Kirk within this Realm,
:fently profested, so long as they keep themfelves
:cietv of Christs Body : And the subfequent *Act* 69.
. declares, That there is none other Face of Kirk,
igion, than was prefently at that time, by the fa-
:d within this Realm,which therefore is ever ftilled,

F

Gods

Gods true Religion , *Chrifts true Religion* , *the true and C*
perfect Religion, Which by manifold Acts of Parliame
Realm are bound to fubfcribe the Articles thereof,
to recant all Doctrine and Errors, repugnant to an
Act 4. and 9. *Parl.* 1. *Act* 45, 46, 47. *Parl.* 3. *Act*
Parl. 7. *Act* 24. *Parl.* 11. *Act* 123. *Par.* 12. *Act* 194.
K. *James* 6. And all Magiftrates, Sherifs, *&c.* O.
dained to fearch, apprehend, and punifh all Co
ftance, *Act* 5. *Parl.* 1. *Act* 104. *Parl.* 7. *Act* 25. P
And that notwithftanding of the King's licences on
are difcharged and declared to be of no force, in f
any wayes, to the prejudice and hinderance of the
of Parliament againft Papifts and Adverfaries of true
Parl. 7. K. *James* 6. On the other part, in the 47. *A*
It is declared and ordained, feing the caufe of Go
his Highnefs Authority are fo joyned, as the hurt o
to both : And that none fhall be reputed as Loyal
to our Soveraign Lord, or his Authority, but be p
and Gain-ftanders of the fame, who fhall not give
make their profeffion of the faid true Religion , ar
ter defection, fhall give the Confeffion of their Fai
promife to continue therein in time coming, to ma
Lords Authority, and at the uttermoft of their po
and maintain the true Preachers and Profeffors o
gainft whatfoever Enemies and Gain-ftanders of the
againft all fuch (of whatfoever Nation, Eftate .
that have joyned, and bound themfelves, or have
fet forward, and execute the cruel Decrees of *Tr*
Preachers and true Profeffors of the Word of Go
word by word in the Article of Pacification at *Perth*
Approved by Parliament the laft of *April* 1573. R
1587. And related, *Act* 123. *Parl.* 12. of K. *James*
That they are bound to refift all treafonable Upro
ed againft the true Religion, the Kings Majefty, anc
Likeas all Liedges are bound to maintain the Ki
Perfon, and Authority, the Authoritie of Parl.
which neither any Laws or lawful Judicatories can b
Act 131. *Parl.* 8 K. *James* 6. And the Subjects I
only to live and be governed by the Kings Laws, t

ly, *Act* 48. *Parl.* 3. K. *James* the firſt, *Act* 79. *Parl.*
peated in the *Act* 131. *Parl.* 8. King *James* 6.
e innovated or prejudged, the Commiſſion anent
two Kingdoms of *Scotland* and *England* , which
the 17. *Parl.* of King *James* the 6. Declares ſuch
inſue, as this Realm could be no more a free Mo-
the fundamental Laws, ancient Priviledges, Offi-
this Kingdom, not only the Princely Authority of
i deſcent hath been theſe many Ages maintained, but
urity of their Lands, Livings, Rights, Offices, Li-
ies preſerved, and therefore for the preſervation of
on, Laws, and Liberties of this Kingdom, it is ſta-
rl. 1. repeated in the 99 *Act Parl.* 7. ratified in the 23
.. *Act Parl.* 12. of K. *James* 6 & 4 *Act* of K. *Charles* 1.
Princes at their Coronation and Reception of their
, ſhall make their faithful Promiſe by their Solemn
e of the Eternal God, That, during the whole time
' ſhall ſerve the ſame Eternal God to the uttermoſt
ording as He has required in His moſt Holy Word,
l and New Teſtament. And according to the ſame
ain the true Religion of Chriſt Jeſus, the Preaching
, the due and right miniſtration of the Sacraments,
reached within this Realm (according to the Con-
nediatly preceeding) and ſhall aboliſh and gain-ſtand
ontrary to the ſame, and ſhall rule the People com-
rge, according to the Will and Command of God,
laid Word, and according to the laudable Laws and
ed in this Realm, no wayes repugnant to the ſaid
God; and ſhall procure, to the uttermoſt of their
of God, and whole Chriſtian People, true and per-
: coming: And that they ſhall be careful to root out
Hereticks, and Enemies to the true Worſhip of God,
ted by the true Kirk of God, of the foreſaid crimes,
rved by*his Majeſty at his Coronation in   *K. *Charles*
nay be ſeen in the order of the Coronation.   the fiſt.
to the Commandment of G O D , conform
the Godly in former times , and according to the
: of our Worthy and Religious Progenitors,
was warranted alſo by Act of *Council*, commanding
be made and ſubſcribed by his Majeſties Subjects, of

all

all Ranks, for two caufes: One was, For defending the true Religion, as it was then reformed, and is expreffed in the Confeffion of Faith above-written, and a former large Confeffion eftablifhed by fundry Acts of lawful *General Affemblies*, and of *Parliaments*, unto which it hath relation, fet down in publick Catechifms, and which had been for many years with a Bleffing from Heaven preached, & profeffed in this Kirk and Kingdom, as *Gods* undoubted Truth, grounded only on His *written Word*. The other caufe was, for maintaining the Kings Majefty, his Perfon, and Eftate: The true worfhip of God, and the Kings Authority, being fo ftraitly joyned, as that they had the fame Friends, and common Enemies, and did ftand and fall together. And finally, being convinced in our minds, and confeffing with our mouths, that the prefent and fucceeding Generations in this Land, are bound to keep the forefaid National Oath and Subfcription inviolable. We ———— under-fubfcribing, confidering divers times before, and efpecially at this time, the danger of the true reformed Religion, * of the Kings honour, and of the publick peace of the Kingdom : By the manifold innovations and evils generally contained and particularly mentioned in ----- Supplications, Complaints, and Proteftations, † Do hereby profefs, and before *God*, His Angels, and the World folemnly declare, That, with our whole Hearts we agree and refolve, all the dayes of our life, conftantly to adhere unto, and to defend the forefaid true Religion, and (forbearing the practice of all Novations ‡ introduced in the matter of the Worfhip of God, or approbation of the corruptions of the publick Government of the Kirk, or civil places and power of Kirk-men, * till they be tryed and allowed in free Affemblies, and in Parliaments) to labour by all means lawful to recover the Purity & Liberty of the Gofpel, as it was eftablifhed & profeffed before the forefaid Novations : And becaufe, after due examination, We plainly perceive, & undoubtedly believe, that the Innovations & evils contained in our Supplications, Complaints, and Proteftations have no warrand of the *word of God*, are contrary to the Articles of the forefaid Confeffions, to the intention and meaning of the bleffed Reformers of Religion in this Land, to the above written Acts of Parliament, and do fenfibly tend to the Re-eftablifhing of the Popifh Religion and Tyranny, and to the fubverfion and ruine of the

true

*His Highnefs's honour (by whofe noble enterprife fo fignally countenanced of the Lord, we have obtained this reviving in our bondage)

† Remonftrances, Declarations, & Teftimonies, of old and of late.

‡ Former or latter.

* Or any other Corruptions of the publick Government of the Kirk Prelatick or Eraftian, either tried or to be tried.

† Remonftrances, Declarations, and Teftimonies.

n, and of our Liberties, Laws and Eſtates, We
: foreſaid Confeſſions are to be interpreted, and
d of the foreſaid Novations and Evils, no leſs than
ad been expreſſed in the foreſaid Confeſſions, and
deteſt and abhore them as well as the particular
red therein.   And therefore from the knowledge
r duty to God, to * our King and   *The Govern-
ly worldly reſpect or inducement, to ment and Coun-
ty will ſuffer, wiſhing a further mea- try.
od for this effect, We promiſe, and ſwear by the
our God, to continue in the Profeſſion and Obedi-
eligion : That we ſhal defend the ſame, and reſiſt
ors and Corruptions, according to our Vocation,
f that power that God hath put in our hands, all
And in like manner with the ſame heart, We
d Men, That We have no intention nor deſire to
t may turn to the diſhonour of God, or to the di-
gs Greatneſs and Authority : But † The Civil Ma-
romiſe and ſwear, that we ſhall, to g ſtrates.
ower, with our means and lives, ſtand to the de-
overaign the Kings Majeſty, his Per- ‡ His Highneſs, his
in the Defence and Preſervation of Perſon, and Au-
ion, Liberties, and Laws of the King- thoritr, when
nutual defence and aſſiſtance, every lawfully choſen
in the ſame cauſe of maintaining and eſtabliſhed,
d his Majeſties Authority, with our prem Magiſtrate
lies, our Means, and whole power, over us.
ons whatſoever.   So that whatſoever ſhall be
for that cauſe, ſhall be taken as done to us all in
one of us in particular.   And that we ſhall neither
y ſuffer our ſelves to be divided or withdrawn by
, allurement, or terror from this Bleſſed and Loy-
ſhall caſt in any let or impediment, that may
1 reſolution, as by common conſent ſhall be found
d ends.   But on the contrary, ſhall by all lawful
r and promote the ſame, and if any ſuch dange:
ion be made to us by word or writ, We, and every
reſs it, or if need be, ſhall incontibent make the
may be timeouſly obviated : Neither do we fear
the

the foul afperfions of Rebellion, Combination, or what elle our Adver-faries from their craft or malice would put upon us, feing what we do is fo well warranted,and arifeth from an unfeigned defire to maintain the *Honour of the true Worfhip of God, * the Majefty of our King, and Government. peace of the Kingdom, for the common happinefs of our felves, and the pofterity. And becaufe we cannot look for a Bleffing from God upon our preceedings, except with our Profeffion and Sub-fcription we joyn fuch a Life and Converfation, as befeemeth Chriftians, who have renewed their Covenant with God ; We therefore,faithfully promife for our felves, our followers and all other under us, both in publick, in our particular Families, and perfonal carriage,to endeavour to keep our felves within the bounds of Chriftian liberty, and to be good Examples to others of all Godlinefs, Sobernefs,and Righteoufnefs, and of every duty we owe to God and Man ; And that this our Union, and Conjunction may be obferved without violation, we call the *Living God, the Searcher of our Hearts* to witnefs, who knoweth this to be our fin-cere Defire, and unfaigned Refolution, *As We fhall anfwer to Jefu Chrift, in the Great Day,* and under the pain of Gods Everlafting Wrath, and of Infamy, and lofs of all honour and refpect in this World. Moft hum-bly befeeching the Lord to ftrengthen us by his holy Spirit for this end, and to blefs our Defires and Proceedings with a happy fuccefs, that Re-ligion and Righteoufnefs may flourifh in the Land, to the Glory of God, † Of our Sove-the honour † of the King,and peace and comfort of us all. raigns. In witnefs whereof, we have fubfcribed with our hands all the Premiffes, &c.

This Article of the Covenant, which was at the firft Subfcription, ‡ Anno 1638. ‡ referred to the determination of the General Affembly, being determined, and thereby the 5 Articles of Perth, the Government of the Kirk by Bifhops, the Civil places and power of Kirk-men, upon the reafons and grounds contained in the Acts of the General Affembly, declared to be unlawful within this Kirk, We fubfcribe ac-cording to the determination forefaid.

A
Solemn League and Covenant.

For Reformation,   and Defence of Religion ; ——————

WE ——————— Having before our Eyes the Glory of God,and
the Advancement of the Kingdom of our Lord and Saviour Jesus
Christ, * the Honour and Happiness of the Kings Majesty   * The establish-
and his Posterity, and the true publick Liberty, Safety,   ment & preser-
and Peace of the Kingdoms, wherein every ones private   vation of the Go-
condition is included ; And calling to mind the tracherous   vernment.
and bloody Plots, Conspiracies, Attempts,and practices of the Enemies
of God, against the true Religion and Professors thereof in all places,
especially in these three Kingdoms, ever since the Reformation of Religion, and how much their rage, power, and presumption are of late,
and at this time increased and excercised ; whereof the deplorable estate
of the Church and Kingdom of *Ireland*, the distressed estate of the Church
and Kingdom of *England*, and the *dangerous estate of the Church and
Kingdom of *Scotland*,are present and publick Testimonies: * Distressed.
we have now at last†(after other means of Supplication,Re-   †(After all the
monstrance,Protestation & Suffering) for the preservation   Supplications,
of our selves and our Religion from utter ruine and de-   Remonstrances,
struction, according to the commendable practice of these   Protestations,&
Kingdoms in former times, and the example of Gods   Sufferings of our
People in other Nations, ‡ after mature deliberation re-   Fathers,and our
solved and determined to enter into a mutual and Solemn   own Grievous
League and Covenant: Wherein we all subscribe, and each   Sufferings and
one of us for himself, with our hands lifted up to the Most   Contendings.)
High God, do Swear,   ‡ After all the
    maturity of deli-
    beration that
    1. That we shall sincerely,really and constantly through   our circumstan-
the Grace of God, endeavour in our several places and cal-   ces could allow.
lings, the preservation of the Reformed Religion in the Church of *Scotland*, in Doctrine, Worship, Discipline,and Government, against our
common Enemies ; The Reformation in the Kingdoms of *England* and
    Ireland

Ireland, in Doctrine, Worship, Discipline, and Government, according to the Word of God, and the example of the best reformed Churches; And shall endeavour to bring the Churches of God in the three Kingdoms to the nearest conjunction and Uniformity in Religion, Confession of Faith, Form of Church Government, Directory for Worship and Catechizing ; That we and our posterity after us, may, as Brethren, live in Faith and Love, and the Lord may delight to dwell in the midst of us.

2. That we shall in like manner, without respect of persons, endeavour the extirpation of Popery, Prelacy, (that *is*, Church goverment by Arch-bishops, Bishops, their Chancellours Commissaries, Deans, Deans and Chapters, Arch-deacons, and all other Ecclesiastical Officers depending on that Hierarchy) Superstition, Heresie, Schism, Prophanness, and whatsoever shall be found to be contrary to sound Doctrine, and the power of Godlinesss; Lest we partake in other Mens sins, and thereby be in danger to receive of their plagues, and that the Lord may be one, and His Name one in the three Kingdoms.

3. We shall with the same sincerity, reality and constancy, in our several Vocations, endeavour with our Estates and Lives, mutually to preserve the Rights and Priviledges of the Parliaments, and the Liberties * The Civil Ma- of the Kingdom ; And to preserve and defend * the Kings gistrates Person Majesties Person and Authority, in the preservation and and Authority. defence of the true Religion, and the Liberties of the Kingdoms; That the World may bear witness with our Consciences of our Loyalty, and that we have no thoughts or intention to diminish his just power and greatness.

4. We shall also with all faithfulness endeavour the discovery of all such as have been, or shall be Incendiaries, Malignants, or evil Instruments, by hindering the Reformation of Religion, dividing † the King † Between the from his People, or one of the Kingdoms from another, Magistrate and or making any faction, or parties amongst the people con-Subjects. trary to this League and Covenant. That they may be brought to publick trial, and receive condigne punishment, as the degree of their offences shall require or deserve, or the Supreme Judicatories of both Kingdoms respectively, or others having power from them for that effect, shall judge convenient.

5. And whereas the happiness of a blessed Peace between these Kingdoms, denied in former times to our Progenitors, is by the good Pro-‡ W•t in the vidence of God granted unto , and ‡ hath been lately dayes of our Fa- concluded , and settled by both Parliaments, We shall thers concluded. each one of us, according to our place and interest, endeavour

:main ‡ conjoyned in a firm Peace & ‡ As they were
, and that Juſtice may be done upon then.
creof, in manner expreſſed in the precedent Article.
cording to our places and callings in this common
berty, and Peace of the Kingdoms, aſſiſt and de-
:r into this League and Covenant, in the main-
hereof; And ſhall not ſuffer our ſelves directly or
ver Combination, Perſwaſion or Terrour, to be
wn from this bleſſed Union and Conjunction,
ſtion to the contrary part, or to give our ſelves to
:y or neutrality in this cauſe, which ſo much con-
God, the good of the Kingdoms, and honour
ll all the dayes of our lives zealouſly   † Of the Go-
e therein, againſt all oppoſition, and vernment.
rding to our power, againſt all Lets and Impe-
And, what we are not able our ſelves to ſuppreſs
. reveal and make known, that it may be timely
l: All which we ſhall do as in the ſight of God.
Kingdoms are guilty of many ſins and provocati-
his Son Jeſus Chriſt, as is too manifeſt by our
igers, the fruits thereof, We profeſs and declare
rld, our unfained deſire to be humbled for our own
: theſe Kingdoms, eſpecially that we have not, as
ineſtimable benefit of the Goſpel, that we have
urity and power thereof, and that we have not
Chriſt in our hearts, nor to walk worthy of him
are the cauſes of other ſins and tranſgreſſions ſo
igſt us, and our true and unfained purpoſe, deſire,
ſelves, and all others under our power & charge,
private, in all duties we ow to God and Man, to a-
ich one to go before another in the example of a
ıat the Lord may turn away his wrath, and heavy
liſh theſe Churches and Kingdoms in truth and
:nant we make in the preſence of Almighty God
ts, with a true intention to perform the ſame. As
eat day, when the ſecrets of all hearts ſhall be
ıbly beſeeching the Lord to ſtrengthen us by his
d, and to bleſs our deſires, and proceedings with
a deliverance and ſafety to his People, and en-

G   coura-

couragement to other Chriſtian Churches, groaning under, or in danger o
the yoke of Antichriſtian Tyranny, or to joyn in the ſame or like Aſ
ſociation and Covenant, to the Glory of God, the enlargement of th
Kingdom of Jeſus Chriſt, and the peace and tranquillity of Chriſtiaſ
Kingdoms, and Common wealths.

Theſe Covenants abovewritten, formerly Nationally Taken and Renewed, an
ſtill Nationally Binding, We, in our private Station only, Swear and Sub
ſcribe in their genuine ſenſe, conform to the Explination and Application there
of, in our preſent Acknowledgement of the publick Sins and Breache
of the ſame, and Engagement to the Duties *contained therein, whic*
do in a ſpecial way relate to the preſent times, and are proper for our capa
ties therein.

A Solemn *Acknowledgement* of

PUBLICK SINS,

AND

BREACHES OF THE COVENANT

AND

A Solemn *Engagement* to all the DUTIES contained
therein, namely theſe which do in a more ſpecial way
relate unto the dangers of theſe times. *Anno* 1689.

WE all, and every one of us—by the good hand of God upon us, taking
ſerious conſideration, the many ſad afflictions, and deep diſtreſ
wherewith we have been exerciſed for a long time paſt. And remember
that as the Land, in the dayes of our Fathers, was ſore waſted, with the Swe
and the Peſtilence, and threatned with Famine, for their Breacnes of Cc
nant ſhortly after they firſt entered into it. For which, Shame & Contempt was pou
out from the Lord againſt many thouſands of our Nation, when they dic
a ſinful way make War upon the Kingdom of *England,* in the year 1648. Cc
trary to the Teſtimony of His Servants, and deſires of His People, and
remnant of that Army returning to this Land, ſpoiled & oppreſed ma
of the Faithful, at that time. And after our Fathers in their Solemn Acknowledgemen
Sins, and Engagement to Duties, had confeſſed the guilt of that Malignant Aſſociation,

obliged themfelves for the future, never any more to connive at, comply with, or countenance Malignancy; Yet they joyned themfelves again with the people of thefe abominations:
And upon terms deftructive to the Nations and Churches Intereft, difhonourable to God, and
prejudicial to Pofterity, accepted their mock Repentance, and admitted Malignants to places
of Power and Truft: And by a precipitant Treaty at Breda with the head of them Charles II.
brought him over and made him King, upon his mock-fubfcription of the Covenant, notwithftanding he had given manifeft difcoveries of his Treachery and Enmity to Religion and
Liberty, in his Commiffionating James Graham to invade this Kingdom, in the mean time of
the Treaty; Whereby God was mocked, his Church cheated, and the State betrayed. And
then a woful defection and divifion was caufed, and carried on, by the Promoters and Abetters of the *Publick Refolutions*, who, notwithftanding the Malignant Party was
ftill numerous, and retaining their former Principles, waited for an opportunity to raife a new and dangerous War, not only to the rending
of the bowels of this Kingdom, but unto the dividing them from England, and overturning of the Work of God in all the three Kingdoms;
did yet intertain and encourage them in their Armies. For which breaches of Covenant, the
anger of the Lord was evidently feen to fmoke againft the Land; which, after the Defeat at
Dunbar and at Worcefter, was brought in fubjection to the Englifh, for feveral years. So in
procefs of time, calling to mind how the Malignants, again recovering power and reftored
to the Government, were fuffered peaceably at their own pleafure and leafure to overturn
the Glorious Work of our *Covenanted Reformation*, and to cut down the carved work of the
Houfe of our God, as it were with Axes and Hammers, by refcinding all the Acts and Laws
made in favours thereof, and to reintroduce the abjured yokes of *Anti-chriftian* Prelacy, *Eraftian*
Supremacy, and *Abfolute Tyranny*; Which, through our finful and fcandalous Complyance
therewith, have been fo far advanced, that there wanted little to the re-eftablifhment of
Popery it felf in thefe Lands. Having it alfo in recent memory, what indignities have been
done to our Covenants, in not only breaking them, and declaring them void and of no force, &
enacting the breaches of them, and abjuring of them, but in burning them, and making it
a capital Crime to own them. Which horrid violations and villanies have been generally
complyed with, or connived at without control. For which, we cannot but acknowledge
and adore the Righteoufnefs of the Lord, in giving us up unto, and fuffering us long to houl
under many miferies and calamities of graffant Tyranny, Oppreffion, Perfecution, and
Murdering violence, thefe Eight and Twenty years: Whereby the Land hath been reduced
almoft to defolation. And confidering alfo, that a cloud of calamities do
ftill hang over our heads, and threaten us with fad things to come, we
cannot but look upon thefe things as from the Lord, who is righteous
in all his wayes, feeding us with the bread of tears, and making us to
drink the waters of affliction, until we be taught to know how evil and
bitter a thing it is to depart away from him, by breaking the Oath and
Covenant which we had made with Him, and that we may be humbled before Him, by confeffing of our fin, and forfaking the evil of our
way.

Therefore being preffed with fo great neceffities and ftraits, and warranted by the word of God, and having the example of Gods People of
old, who in the time of their troubles, and when they were to feek de-

livery

livery, and a right way for themselves , that the
them to prosper them, did humble themselves bef
a free and particular confession of the sins of their I
their Captains, their Priests, and their People : A:
selves to do no more so, but to reform their wayes, :
Covenant. And remembring the practice of our
year 1596. wherein the *General Assembly* and all th
with the concurrence of many of the Nobility, C
les , did with many tears acknowledge before (
the National Covenant, and engaged themselv
on , even as our Predecessors and theirs had
the *General Assembly* and Convention of States ,
And the more recent practice of the Godly renewing the *National* C
ing the breaches of it , both before they obtained Authority, for i
again by Authority, in the year 1639. And that noble Preceden
Acknowledgement of *Publick Sins*, and Breaches of the Solemn L
Solemn Engagement to all the *Duties* contained therein (which we
scended upon by the Commission of the General Assembly , appt
Estates , and publickly owned in all the Churches , at the renewi
anno 1648. and 1649. Together with the Solemn Renovation tl
such confession of Sins as did suit that time, yet fresh in our mem
of the LORDS People, at *Lanerk*, before their discomfiture at P
ceiving that this Duty, when gone about out of C
often been attended with a reviving out of trouble
and Success from Heaven : We do humbly an
sight who is the searcher of hearts, Acknowledge
great transgressions of the Land : We have done w
our Princes, our Nobles, our Judges, our Officers
our People. Albeit the Lord hath long and clear
have not hearkned unto His voice : Albeit He h:
tender mercies , we have not been allured to wait t
in His way : And thô He hath stricken us, yet we ha
thô He hath consumed us, we have refused to rec
have not remembred to render unto the Lord ac
ness, and according to our Vows and Promises ;
backward , by a continued course of backsliding.
and shamefully broken the National Covenant, and all th
lemn League and Covenant, which our Fathers swo
gels and Men.
  Albeit there be in the Land some of all ranks,
mony to the Truth, and for a name of Joy and I

ftudying to keep their **Garments** pure, and being
nant and Gaufe of God ; Yet we have reafon to ac-
t of us have not endeavoured with that reality, fin-
:y, that did become us, to preferve the work of Re-
irk of *Scotland.* · As we are obliged by the 1. *Article* of the So-
nt, and by the National Covenant, wherein we Promife and Swear
the Lord our God, that we fhall continue in the obedience of the
of this Kirk, and fhall defend the fame accordirg to our Vocat on
of our Lives, under the pains contained in the Law, and danger
in the day of Gods fearful Judgement ; And refift all contrary Er-
.ccording to our Vocations, and the uttermoft of that power God
Il the dayes of our life : According to thefe Scriptures, *Ezra* 9. 10.
Dan. 7. 25. *Gal.* 5. 1. I *Tim.* 4. 16. 2 *Tim.* 1, 13. *Rev.* 3.
fo far from fuch endeavours, that we have ftupidly fubmmitted
aes breaking down and overturning the whole Work of Reforma.
thereof, refcinding the Laws in favours of the fame, and not on-
he Covenants for preferving it, enacting the Breaches thereof, and
iereof void, and criminal to be owned ; And upon the ruines thereof
a, Eraftian Prelacy, with its concomitant bondage of Patronages,
s Supremacy, and Arbitrary Power in the Magiftrate, over Church
e confcience of conftant endeavours to preferve the Reformation,
n teftifie againft thofe audacious and Heaven-daring Attempts.
y a wicked Edict ejected from their Charges, both they and the
i with it. And albeit in the National Covenant we are obliged
on, and to labour by all means lawful to recover the Purity and Li-
bearing the practifes of all Novations introduced in the Worfhip of
the Corruptions of the Publick Government of the Kirk ; Yet
n required by Law of the Novation, and corruption of Prelacy, by
tes. We and our Teachers in a great meafure complyed with,
ved at the encroachments of the Supremacy and Abfolute Power,
untenancing the former Indulgences, and the late Tolleration.
ibed Oaths and Bonds, all which have been impofed thefe
reffing Conformity with the prefent Eftablifhments of Church and
unto the Reformation we fwore to preferve : Some of them re-
fours to preferve it, as thofe that renounced the Priviledge of De-
em Abjuring the Covenants exprefly, and condemning the pro-
, as Rebellion, viz. The *Declaration* and *Teft.* We have *Iffachar*-
lens, in maintaining and defending an Arbitrary Power, and Ab.
ployed and applied for the deftruction of the Reformation, and
upplies as were declaredly impofed for upholding of Tyrants U-
; all endeavours to preferve the Reformation. We have not con-
otain the Doctrine of this Reformed Church : Many of our Mi.
furceafed from bearing witnefs to fome perfecuted Truths, and
ie to the fins and corruptions of the Times ; Whereby many of
ome with fnares, and left to feek and maintain other Principles
complyance, or extravagance on the right and left hand, not
: and Rules of the Church of *Scotland* : Others of us have been
not conftant in confeffing them before men, when called to
lafti

suffer for and avouch them : Hypocritical, in profeſſing them ,
and converſation becoming the Goſpel. Cauſe, and Croſs of *ch*
Controverted, than the Fundamental and Practical Truths of C
ſhort in Real. Sincere and conſtant endeavours to preſerve the
and Private : Many of our Miniſters have left off Preaching ,
times of hazard : We have been negligent and remiſs in Family
preſerving it , many of us have done much to diſcourage and b
And in ſecret Worſhip we have been Formal and careleſs.

themſelves with the Purity of the Ordinances ,
thereof ; yea, ſome have turned aſide to crooked
both. We have not been careful to preſerve the Diſcipline
Cenſures being laid aſide , and not impartially exerciſed ag:
publick : Scandalous perſons being admitted to hold up their C
the Communion of the Lords Table, and other priviledges of th
the Rules of *Chriſt*, or conſtitution of this Church : And many
giving, in taking, and removing Offences, without obſerving th
And ſome inclining ſometimes to wayes tending either to the dif
Uſurpation of an Independent or Popular way of exerciſing it
firſt *Article* of the Solemn League, we are bound to *endeavour th*
the Reformation, and Uniformity in Religion, Confeſſion of Faith
(which as it was primarly underſtood, ſo ſtill we owne to be on
Worſhip and Catechiſing; According to Scripture, *Iſa.* 19. 18.
Act. 2. 46. 1 *Cor.* 7. 17 *Ibil.* 3. 16. *Gal.* 6. 16. Yet, a
complain that The profane, looſe and inſolent Car
Armies who went to the aſſiſtance of our Brethre
tamperings and unſtraight dealings of ſome Com
our Nation, in *London*, the Iſle of *Wight*, and oth
dom, had proved, great Lets to the Work of Ref
of Kirk Government there, whereby Error and S
been encreaſed, and Sectaries hardened in their w
day, we are obliged to confeſs the Offenſive Carriage and Con
gone to *England*, who have proven very ſtumbling to the Sectar
perings of others, in patching up an Union and Communion wi
againſt their way : And on the other band, we have had little
ſuch an Uniformity ; Little praying for it ; And little mourning f
of late, many have embraced a Toleration, introductive of a S
ligions, without ſo much as a Teſtimony againſt the Toleratio

In the II. *Article*. We are bound, without reſpect of perſo
tion of *Popery*, conform to the National Covenant, where w
" deteſt all kind of Papiſtry, in general and particular heads,
" and confuted by the Word of God, and Kirk of *Scotland*. Like
" not only in general, do abrogate all Laws, Statutes and Conſt
" the true Religion, and Profeſſors thereof, or of the true Kirk
" Freedom thereof, or in favours of the Popiſh Idolatry and Su
" conſtitute, enact, ratifie and aprove, many Penal Statute
founded upon Divine Precepts and other *Scriptures*, *Exod.* 23

Ig. 2. 2. Zech. 13. 2. 3. 1 Tim. 4. 1, 2, 3. 2 Theff. 2. 3.
. 18. 4, 5, 6. Yet, alas! We have been fo defective in this,
e Land hath been polluted again with Idolatrous Maffes; Alters,
peen fuffered to be again erected; Penal Statutes have been fo
inft Papifts, that they have been by Arbitrary and Abfolute Pow-
nd difabled by the Toleration, in its own nature tending, and
oduce Popery and Slavery; Yet this hath been accepted and ad-
lers, and countenanced, complyed, and concurred with, by
timony; or endeavour to withftand it. Yea the Adminiftration of
Offices of Power and Truft, hath been committed to, & permitted
fts: And the Head of them, & great Pillar & Promoter of Popery,
wned as King, contrary to the Laws of God and Man, which inca-
nt obligations; without refpect of perfons, to extirpate Papifts.
ttle Zeal or Indignation againft, or fear of the manifeft appear-
pery, and intended Eftablifhment of it in the Land; And little
ine and fall of Babylon, and that the Lord would divide and over-
otters thereof. Many, on the contrary, have prayed for Bleffings
ent of a Papift on the Throne, the chiefeft Supporter of it in thefe
We were bound "*To endeavour the Extirpation of* Prelacy, *that is,*
bifhops, Bifhops, their Chancellours, and Commiffaries, Deans, Deans
d all other Ecclefiaftical Officers, depending on that Hierarchy; As in the
ohor and deteft the Antichriftian wicked Hierarchie, and to forbear
ons, and approbation of the Corruptions of the publick Govern-
og contrary to the Article of the forfaid Confeffion, to the inten-
ffed Reformers of Religion in this Land, and to Acts of Parliament
tending to the re-eftablifhing of the Popifh Religion and Tyranny,
uine of the true reformed Religion, & of our Liberties, Laws, &
cerning Prelacy, being referred to the General Affembly, was deter-
rful, as being clearly condemned in the Word of God. Math 20. 25.
B. 20. 17. 28, 1 Pet. 5 3. 3 Job. 9. Yet we have been fo
lows, that Prelacy hath been by wicked Law eftabl.fhed; and in
been fubmitted unto, and complied with by us; And in evidence
by wicked and Arbitrary Laws, we heard, and received Ordr-
ruding Curats, and payed them Stipends and Emoluments, exact-
h we were bound to extirpate. And not only fo, but many did
s, by Subfcription, Promife, or Oath, to be ordinary Church-
Church: And all of us, even the we did ftand at a diftance from,
Faction; yet we became very remifs in our Zeal, and flack in our
I nftead of endeavours to extirpate *Superftition* and *Herefie*, as
Article of the Solemn League, and by the National Covenant, "to
nd Herefies, without, or againft the Word of God, and Doctrine
According to the Scriptures, Deut. 12. 30, 31, 32. Act. 17 22.
ol 2. 20, 21, 23. Tit. 3. 10. Yet in the darknefs of thefe times,
rftition have been obferved, many Omens and F.rets, too much
il dayes, as Pafch, Yule, Faftens-even. &c. have been kept by many;
y-dayes and Feftivities devifed of their own heart, appointed for
gs Birth dayes, as May 29. and October 14. &c. who were both as
lave been complyed with by many. Yet fome have fuperftiticufly
, as a Fortune-book, looking to that which was firft caft up to
them,

them, or to Impreſſions Born in upon their minds, from ſuch and ſuch parts of Scripture, as Divine Reſponſes, with out a due ſearch of them, as the Lord hath commanded. And, many wavering and unſtable, have been ſeduced into damnable and pernicious Hereſies, as *Quakers*, and delirious deluſiont of ſuch as followed *John Gibb*. All which have been Breaches of Covenant, as well as Divine Commands: Yet Hereſies of all kinds have been Tolerated, yea encouraged in our day, without a witneſs againſt them from many. Moreover, we are, bound in our Covenant, to oppoſe & extirpate *Schiſm* on the one hand, as well as *Defection* on the other; The Scripture makes this a great ſin, *Rom.* 16. 17. 1*Cor.* 11. 18. 1*Cor.* 12. 25. *Heb.* 12, 25. *Jud. v.* 19. Yet, as many by defection, both in complyance with Prelacy and Eraſti. aniſm, have broken the Churches Beauty and Bands, Order and Union, in making a Faction; repugnant to her eſtabliſhed Order, and Cenſurable by all her ſtanding Acts, in bringing in Novations in the Government, and making a rent in the Bowels of the Church, by cauſing Diviſions and Offences, contrare to the Doctrine of the Church, have made themſelves guilty of Schiſm: So, others on the other hand, have, upon ſlender and inſuf-

*Meaning, ſuch Miniſters as were moſt faithful and zealous, preached in the Fields, and were not chargeable with Defection and Complyance with Enemies; From whom ſome ſeparate, as *John Gibb*, and others·

ficient grounds, ſeparate, both from *Miniſters, from Chriſtian Societies, and Families, becauſe of differences in judgement, in incident debates, not neceſſary nor material, nor wherein the Teſtimony of Chriſt was much concerned, or becauſe of perſonal Offences, eaſily removed; Not obſerving the Rules of Chriſt for removing them, nor having reſpect to His great Commands of Charity, Forbearance, Forgiving one another, or Condeſcendency. And, between divided parties, which in our day, have long been byting and devouring one another, there hath been too much, both of ſinful Union and Confederacy, in termes prejudicial to Truth and Duty, on the one hand; and of ſinful heats, Animoſities, Jealouſies, Pride, Paſſion and Prejudices, on the other hand; grieving the Spirit of God, and eating up the Power, and much hindering the holy Practice and Spiritual Exerciſe of Religion. And too much alſo of ſowing diſcords among Brethren, and promoting our contentions by too credulous and ſedulous taking up, & ſpreading reports and reproaches one of another. What ſhall we ſay? We have been ſo far from endeavouring the extirpation of Profanneſs (another evil engaged againſt in the Covenant and condemned in the Word of God, *Deut.* 29. 19. *Job*, 21. 14. *Jer.* 23. 15 *Ezek* 22 26. *Hoſ.* 4. 1, 2, 3. *Heb.* 12. 15. 16) that Profanity hath been much winked at, and profane perſons much countenanced, and many times employed, until Iniquity & Ungodlineſs hath gone over the face of the Land as a flood: Nay ſufficient care hath not been had, to ſeparate betwixt the precious and the vile, by debarring from the Sacrament all ignorant and ſcandalous perſons, according to the Ordinances of this Kirk. And hence it hath come to paſs, that Profanity beginning at the Court and corrupt Clergy, and deſcending from them like a flood, hath overſpread the whole Land; So that the greateſt part by far, may rather be called Children of *Sodom*, then of a land ſolemnly in Covenant with God: And ſo far have we been from rooting out whatſoever is contrary to ſound Doctrine and the power of Godlineſs, left we partake of other mens ſins, and be in danger to receive of their plagues, that we have maintained much unſound Doctrine in the Arguments which we uſed for defence of our courſes of complyance with Prelacy and Eraſtianiſm, and walking willingly after

after the Commandments of Men : And thofe, among others, unfound Notions have been intertained among us ; *That leſſer and circumflantial Truths are not to be ſuffered for ; That con-feſſion of theſe Truths hath not been called for in our day ; That People are not in hazard of the ſins of others, eſpecially Magiſtrates and Miniſters, if they do not directly Act the ſame ſins them-ſelves ;* contrary to expreſs and plain Scriptures, 2 Sam. 21. 1. 2 Sam. 24. 17. 2 Kings 21. 11, 12. Lev. 10. 6 Iſai. 43. 27, 28, Jer: 14. 15, 16. Micah 3. 11, 12. Whence both Mini-ſters and People have been involved in the ſins of Prelacy, Indulgence and Tolleration, thinking theſe only the ſins of Prelates, and of Uſurping Rulers, while they yeelded all the Conformity with them, ſubmiſſion to them, and approbation of them, that was required by wicked Laws. On the other hand, many of us have reſted too much in Non-comply-ance with theſe, and having a form of Godlineſs, but neglecting the power thereof.

In the Third Article, whereas we are bound in our ſeveral Vocations. *To endeavour with our Eſtates and Lives, mutually to preſerve the Rights and Priviledges of Parliament, and Liberties of the Kingdoms,* meaning true real and righteous Priviledges and Liberties, conſonant to the Word of God, Deut. 1. 13. Deut. 16. 16. Iſa. 1. 26. "Like as all Liedges are bound by " the Laws of the Land, inſert in the National Covenant, to maintain the Authority of Par- "liaments, without which, neither any Laws, or lawful Judicatories can be eſtabliſhed : Yet, as our Fathers found reaſon to complain, that neither had the Priviledges of the Par-liaments and Liberties of the Subject been duely tendered, but ſome a-mongſt them had laboured to put into the hands of the King an Arbitrary and Unlimited Power deſtructive to both, and many of them had been acceſſory to those means and wayes whereby the freedom and privi-ledges of Parliaments had been encroached upon, and the Subjects op-preſſed in their Conſciences, Perſons and Eſtates ; So, in our day, ſince this long tract of Tyranny began, they have had rather the name and ſhew, than the real Pow-er and Priviledges of lawful by conſtitute Parliaments, ſince they advanced the Regal Pre-rogative to ſuch a boundleſs pitch of Abſoluteneſs ; Being ſo corrupted, that faithful Men, and honeſt and honourable Patriots have been excluded, and thoſe admitted for conſtituent Members, that by the Law of God and Man ſhould have been debarred. And ſo prelimi-ted, that the Members behooved to take ſuch Oaths, for inſtance the *Declaration* and *Teſt*, abjuring and condemning the Covenants, as engaged them to be perjured and conjured E-nemies both to our Religion and Liberty ; Which was ſinfully complyed with, both by the Electors of Parliament-Members, and by the Elected. Yet the body of the Land did not make conſcience of endeavouring the recovery of theſe Rights and Priviledges ſo perverted and polluted. Whence nothing could flow from theſe Fountains ſo poyſoned, but injuſtice and oppreſſion ; And in ſtupid ſubmiſſion did own theſe for their Repreſentatives who be-trayed their Liberties, and made Laws to enſlave the Nation, and entail Slaverie on the Poſterity. On the other hand, we that diſowned them did not mind the Duty of preſerving theſe Rights and Priviledges of Supreme Judicatories, when inadvertently and unadviſed-ly we put in ſuch Expreſſions and Stiles in ſome of our *Declarations*, that do not belong to private Perſons, but to ſuch Judicatories. Again, the *Subjects Liberties*, Civil and Religious, both as Men and as Chriſtians, which the Scriptures allow we ſhould preſerve, 1 Sam: 14: 45: Acts 22: 25: Acts 25: 11, 16, 27. Gal: 5. 1. have been miſerably encroached on by Ar-bitrary Government, whereby the Subjects have been oppreſſed in their Conſciences, Perſons, and E-ſtates, by all the Oaths and Bonds preſſing Conformity with theſe Corruptions, Novations, and Uſurpations in the Government of Church and State ; And perſecutions for Recuſancy, and by impoſitions on the Natural freedom of ſecret thoughts, which no law of Man can reach, yet in our day extorted by threatnings of Torture and Death, if they were not diſcovered in

Anſwers

Anfwerstoour perfecuters impertinent queftions. In all which i
ties as men, we have too ftupidly couched under all burdens, a
The Churches Liberties have alfo been invaded by the Ecclefiafti
by a Blafphemous Law inherent in the Crown, and by an Abfolu
required to obey without referve, which are horrid encroachn
cable *Prerogatives* of JEHOVAH, and His CHRIST as only King
And yet thefe have been eftablifhed and homologated by our feve
of Prelacy, and its attending Patronages, robbing the Church of
Paftors; Indulgence and Tolleration; to the prejudice of, and
Churches Liberties. In that fame *Article*, we are bound alfo t
*preme Magiftrates Perfon and Authority, in the prefervation and defe
Liberties of the Kingdoms*. As in the National Covenant is expreff:
"Perfon and Authority, in the defence of Chrift his Evangel,]
"Miniftration of Juftice and punifhment of iniquity; and ftand (
"fence and prefervation of the forefaid true Religion, Liberties a
As the Duty is qual:fied in Scriptures, 2 *Sam:* 5: 3; 2 *Kings* 11: 17:
26: 16, 21: *Rom:* 13: 3, 4: 1 *Pet:* 2: 14. But as our Fathers in th
reafon to fay, Neither hath it been our care to avoic
might harden the King in his evil way; But upo
hath not only been perinitted, but many of us hav
to make him exercife his Power in many things ten
of Religion and of the Covenant, and of the Peac
Kingdoms; Which is fo far from the right way (
jefties Perfon and Authority, that it cannot but
gainft him, unto the hazard of both; Nay, undei
ing and doing for the King, whilft he refules to d(
for the Houfe of God, fome have ranverfed and vi
Articles of the Covenant. So, in our unhappy dayes, it
row, that we have had to do with men mouned on a Throne of in
verting Religion and Perfecuting it, defigning to introduce
Slaverie, Deftroying our Liberties, Suppreffing the Evan
Profeffors, Enacting and Executing manifeft Injuftice, (t
Juftice againft Idolaters, Adulterers, Murderers, and
and punifhing Equity and Duty inftead of Iniquity, arrogating a
Prerogative above all Rights and Priviledges of Parliament,
power to Tyrannize as he lifts without control. But, as it was ou
the late King, after fuch difcoveries of his Hypocritical emoity to
on his fubfcription of the Covenant; So, whin he burnt and b
degenerate into manifeft Tyrannie, and had razed the very found
Right to govern, and the Peoples Allegiance were founded,.
Allegiance by annulling the Bond of it; We finned in continuin{
when oppofite to and deftructive of Religion and Liberty. And i
of *Allegiance* (including alfo the *Supremacy* with the boundlefs
Reftrictions or Qualifications, when all the Authority he had w
a Rebellion againft God, forgetting, foregoing and difowning
venant; And in putting in his Intereft (with the Application of (

him, thô ſtated in oppoſition to it) in the ſtate of the quatrel, in our *Declarations* of war
Pentland and *Bothuel-Bridge*, for which the Lord put us to ſhame, and went not out with
ir Armies. Again we deſire to confeſs and mourn over this as the ſin of the Land, and
each of Covenant, that the Duke of *York* hath been admitted to the exerciſe of the Royal
ffice, againſt the Laws of God and man, being incapable of the Covenants qualificaticor
a Magiſtrate, and, being a *Papiſt*, incapable of taking the Oath of *Coronation*, to main-
in the True *Proteſtant Religion*, and aboliſh and gainſtand *Popery*; which, for the preſer-
ition of the *true Religion*, Laws and Liberties of this Kingdom, is ſtatute by the 8 *Act*
Irl: 1: *K*: *J am*: 6: That all Kings at the Reception of their Princely Authority, ſhall take and.
rear.   Yet his Authority, thô inconſiſtent with, and declaredly oppeſite to Religion and
iberty, hath been owned and upheld, by paying the *Ceſs* and *Supplies* expreſly exacted for
aintaining Tyrannie in the deſtruction of Religion and Liberty.

Our own Conſciences within, and *Gods* Judgements upon us without,
o convince us of the manifold wilful renewed Breaches of the *Fourth*
Irticle, which concerneth the diſcovery of Malignants ; conſonant to the
:riptures ; 2 *Sam*: 23: 6:   *Eſther* 7: 5, 6: *Pſal*: 26: 5, 6: *Pſal*: 101: 8: *Prov*: 25: 5: For their
:rimes have not only been connived at, but diſpenſed with and par-
oned, and themſelves received into intimate Fellowſhip----- and en-
:uſted with----- Counſels, admitted into-----Parliaments, and put in
laces of Power and Authority for managing the publick Affairs of
he Kingdom, whereby in *Gods* Juſtice, they got at laſt into their hands
he whole power and Strength of the Kingdom, both in Judicatories
nd Armies; and did imploy the ſame unto the enacting and proſecut-
1g an unlawful Engagement in War againſt the Kingdom of *England* ;
Notwithſtanding of the diſcent of many conſiderable Members of Par-
iament, who had given conſtant proof of their integrity in the Cauſe,
rom the beginning; Of many faithful Teſtimonies, and free Warn-
ngs of the Servants of *God* ; of the Supplications of many *Synods*, *Preſ-*
yteries and *Shires* ; And the Declarations of the *General Aſſembly* and their
Commiſſioners to the Contrary ;   Which Engagement, as it was the
Cauſe of much Sin, ſo alſo of much Miſerie and Calamity unto this Land,
and held forth the grieveouſneſs of our ſin in Complying with Malignants, in the greatneſs of our Judgement, that we may be taught never
:o ſplit again upon the ſame Rock, upon which the Lord hath ſet ſo
Remarkable a beacon.   And after all that is come to paſs unto us, be-
:auſe of this our treſpaſs; And after that Grace hath been ſhewed unto
our Fathers, and us. once and again, from the Lord our God, by breaking
theſe Mens Yoke from off their, and our necks, and ſometimes delivering our
Fathers ſo far from their inſultings, that He put them into a Capacity to Act for
the good of Religion, their own ſafety, and the Peace and ſafety of the
Kingdom, ſhould they and we again break his Commandment and Co-

venant, by joyning once more with the People of thefe Abominations and taking into our bofome thofe Serpents, which had formerly ftung us almoft unto death. This, as it would argue great madnefs and folly upon our part; So, no doubt, if it be not avoided, will provoke the Lord againft us to Confume us, until there be no remnant, nor efcaping in the Land. Many times have we been warned of the Sin of Complyance with Malignants, both by faithful Inftructions, and fatherly Corrections from the Lord; Yet after all thefe Punifhments, and after all thefe Mercies, in mitigating thefe Punifhments, We have again joyned with the People of thefe Abominations. *The Lord is Righteous, for we remain yet efcaped, as it is this day: Behold we are before Him in our Trefpaffes, and we cannot ftand before Him, becaufe of this.* Thefe Incendiaries, Malignants, and evil Inftruments, made many grievous Encroachments, and prevailed much in the dayes of our Fathers; But not without diffent, Teftimonies, Warnings, and Declarations to the Contrary: But, in our unhappy dayes, they have been fuffered, yea encoutaged, without any fignificant joynt Teftimony, not only to hinder the Reformation of Religion, but to overturn the whole Work of Reformation, to Burn and Bury the Covenants for it, to re-eftablifh abjured Prelacy: erect a monftrous, Chrift-exauctorating, and Church-enflaving Supremacy, attempt the introduction of Popery and Slavery at the gate of an Antichriftian Tolleration, and to perfecute and deftroy the Godly, who durft not in confcience comply with them. *And not only to divide the King from his People, or one of the Kingdoms from another*, but, firft to divide the bulk and body of both Kingdoms, and make them purfue divided Interefts, from the Intereft and Caufe of *Chrift*; And then to divide the remnant, of fuch as adhered to it, among themfelves, by *Indulgences*, and other bones of contention, in order to get them more eafily deftroyed; And at length, to engage the King into fuch a divifion from the People, as to make him, inftead of their Protector, their declared Deftroyer: And, not only *to make parties among the People*, contrary to this League and Covenant, but to draw and divide the whole People to party with their perjuries. And yet fo far have we been from endeavours to have them *brought to tryal and condign punifhment, as the fupreme Judicatories of the Kingdom fhould judge convenient*, that they have been fuffered to obtain, and manage the whole Adminiftration of Judgement in their own hands, and to fit and act as the fole Reprefentatives of the Kingdom; Yea, not only have we fuffered them fo to fit and act, but have owned them as our Reprefentatives, in complying with their Mifchiefs framed into Law, in abetting, ftrengthening, and encouraging the Prelatical faction, in their avowed oppofition to the Covenant. The generality have owned Allegiance to the Head of thefe Incendiaries and Malignants, yea a *Popifh Incendiarie*, becaufe he wore a Crown on his head; And have payed the Cefs, impofed for the maintenance and encouragement of Malignants: Many have Affociared with them, in Expeditions of War, drawing up with them in their Mufters, and Rendezvoufes, thereby countenancing a Malignant caufe; and lifting themfelves under a Malignant, yea, *Popifh Banner*: Many have fubfcribed, yea, fworn themfelves of their Faction, contrary to the Covenant, by taking *Tefts, Oaths* and *Bonds*, obliging them to furceafe from Covenanted Duties, and to keep the peace, and good behaviour with them, whom they were obliged by the Covenant, to feek to bring to punifhment: yea fome, and not a few, were inveigled in the fnare of the Oath of *Delation*, to Delate the perfecuted People of God to their Courts, and thereby made, in ftead of d fcovering Malignants, according to the Covenant, to difcovet their Brethren to Malignants: And very many, almoft the univerfality of the Land, were involved in the fnare of the Oath of *Abjuration* renouncing the principle of declaring War againft a *Malignant King*, and of afferting the lawfulnefs of bringing his murdering complyces and Incendiaries to condign punifhment. But, on the other hand, fome of us have

have sometimes exceeded the bounds of Moderation in this matter, in usurping the sword, without Gods Call, without respect to the Rule, and against the scope of our own *Declarations*, to take vengeance on them, at our own hand; yea, even to that degree of taking the Lives of * some of them in an extravagant manner; For which, we have been sadly rebuked of God, and occasion hath been given, and taken, to reproach and blaspheme the Way of *God* upon that account.

* *such as the Curate of Cars-p*harn, *and some others.*

In the 5th *Article*, we are bound according to our peace and Interest, to endeavour that " the Kingdoms may remain Conjoyned in a firm Peace and Union to all Posterity, and " that Justice may be done on the willful opposers thereof ; According to *Gal*. " 5: 12. I*a*. 2. 2 3 I*a* 19. 23. 24. 25. *Jer*. 50. 4, 5. *Ezek* 37 16. 17. *Zech*. 2. 11. *Zech*. 8. 20. 22. 23. But thô the Peace and Union betwixt the King-doms be a great blessing of God unto both, and a Bond which we are obliged to preserve unviolated; And to endeavour that justice may be done upon the opposers thereof; Yet, some in this Land, who have come under the Bond of the Covenant, have made it their great study how to dissolve this Union, and few, or no endeavours, have been used by any of us, for Punishing of such. Yea, very little, or not at all, have the most of us been concerned about this *Article*, whether there be Peace with, or holiness and truth in the other Kingdoms, or what sort of Peace, or on what Foundations it be settled. Both Kingdoms are mutually guilty of dissolving this Covenanted Union, in Invading each other, at several times, contrary to the Covenant: The *English* Nation, in subjecting us to their Conquest, and forcing us to a submission and Union with their *Sectarian* Usurpations, on Church and State: And this Nation, in giving such provocations to them, by the Unlawful Engagement, in the year 1648: By treating with setting up, and entertaining the Head of the Malignant party, their Enemy and ours both, as our King, in the year 1650; And in wading them upon his quarrel, in the *Worcester* expedition, *Anno* 1651. Since which time, after that Kingdom and this both united in that unhappy course of restoring the King, without respect to the Covenant; And re-establishing Prelacy, which broke our Covenanted Union and Conjunction, That Nation hath sometimes sent aid to our Persecutors, for suppressing our Attempts to recover our Religion and Liberties; And this Nation hath sent Forces to help their Destroyers, and to suppress their Endeavours for the recovery of their Priviledges. And in the mean time, we have been very little solicitous for Correspondence to settle Union with such of them as owned the Covenant; Or, for giving to, or receiving from them, mutual Informations of our respective cases and conditions, under all our Calamities and Calumnies cast upon us: Nor have we studied to keep up Sympathie, or Communion of Saints, or a mutual bearing of one anothers burdens, as became Covenanted Brethren. On the other hand, in stead of Union in Truth and Duty, according to the Bond of the Covenant, a Confederacy hath been studied, in Defection from the Covenant: And an Union and Peace, which wanted the foundation laid down in the foregoing Articles of the Covenant, to wit, Uniformity in Doctrine, Worship, Discipline and Government, against *Popery*, *Prelacy*, *Schism*, or *Sectarianism*, for our Religion, Laws, and Liberties, and the discovering, suppressing and punishing the enemies of these Interests. Such an Union hath not been studied or sought; but on the contrare, an Union against the Reformation, and Uniformity for Prelacy, or Sectarian Multiformity, by maintaining Tyranny, and strengthening Malignancy.

In the 6th. *Article*, We are bound, *according to our Places and Callings in this common Cause of Religion, Liberty, and Peace, to assist and defend all those that enter into this League and Covenant, in the maintaining thereof.* And in the National Covenant, in like manner, we are bound "to " stand to the mutual defence and assistance, every one of us of another, in the same cause,

" with

"with our beſt Counſel, our Bodies, Means, and whole Power, againſt all ſorts of perſons "whatſoever; So that whatſoever ſhall be done to the leaſt of us for that Cauſe, ſhould be "taken as done to us all in general, and to every one of us in particular. A duty very clear in the Scriptures, *Judg.* 5. 23. 1 *Chron.* 12. 1, 18. *Nehem.* 4. 14. *Prov.* 24. 11. 12. But alas! Little Conſcience hath been made of this Duty : We have ſuffered many of our Brethren, in ſeveral parts of the Land, to be oppreſſed of the common Enemy, without compaſſion or relief. There hath been great murmur-ing and repining becauſe of expence of means, and pains in doing of our duty. And not only ſo, but many have Sworn and Subſcribed Oaths and Bonds engaging againſt ſuch aſſiſtances very directly, and to condemn all ſuch endeavours to aſſiſt, defend, or reſcue them, as *Sedition* and *Rebellion* ; And obliging them to aſſiſt their murdering Malig-nant Enemies by ſuch concurrences as they required : Yea, many inſtead of coming out to the help of the Lord againſt the Mighty, and defending their Brethren, have come out to the help of the Mighty againſt the Lord, His Cauſe, Covenant and oppreſſed People, concurring in Armes againſt them at all the Appearances that have been aſſayed for the cauſe of Chriſt ; Appearing at Courts, held for informing againſt, and Condemning their Brethren that were Preſent at, or concerned in ſuch Appearances for the Covenanted Cauſe ; And coming in as Witneſſes againſt them; Sitting in Aſſyſes for Condemning them; And guarding them to their Executions, when Martyred for their Duty and the Intereſt of Truth. Many again have denied to Reſet, Harbour, and Entertain their Brethren, Perſecuted for maintaining the Covenanted Reformation ; And ſome have raiſed the *Hue and Cry* after them, thereby occa-ſioning and aſſiſting in the cruel Murder of ſeveral faithful Brethren. The moſt part have owned the Great Murderer, who authorized all the reſt and enacted all theſe Murders; And aſſiſted him and his Complices and Executioners of his murdering Mandats, with their Purſes and Eſtates, in paying the Supplies profeſſedly demanded, and declaredly impoſed for enabl-ing them to accompliſh theſe Miſchiefs. Yea, many of our Brethren have been ſo far from aſſiſting that they have added afflictions to their afflicted Brethren, by their Reproaches, and perſecuting by the Tongue whom the Lord had ſmitten, and talking to the grief of thoſe whom He had wounded. And as all ſorts of us have been wanting in our Sympathie with, and en-deavouring ſuccour to our ſuffering Brethren, let be to deliver them from their Enemies hands, according to capacity, eſpecially if they were ſuch as differed from us in their Judge-ment ; So we cannot forbear with ſhame and ſorrow to confeſs, that many Miniſters have all alongſt diſcovered great unconcernedneſs with, and contempt of poor deſpiſed and reproach-ed Sufferers; Condemning the Heads of their Sufferings; Forgetting, or refuſing to pray for them publickly; And declining, yea, diſſwading to contribute for the relief of the Baniſh-ed, or ſlate; Which hath been very diſcouraging to the afflicted, and ſtumbling to many. In the ſame *Article*, we are bound not to *ſuffer our ſelves directly or indirectly, by whatſoever Com-bination or Terror, to be divided and withdrawn from this bleſſed Union and Conjunction; Whether to make defection to the contrary part, or to give our ſelves unto a deteſtable indifferency or neutrality in this Cauſe.* And in the National Covenant, "That we ſhall neither directly nor indirectly ſuffer "our ſelves to be divided, or withdrawn, by whatſoever ſuggeſtion, allurement or terror "from this Bleſſed and Loyal Conjunction; According to Scripture warrands, *Gen.* 13. 8. *Pſal* 133. throughout. *Zech.* 8. 19. *Heb.* 12. 14. 1 *Cor.* 1. 10. *Eph.* 4. 3. *Phil.* 1. 27. and 2. 1, 2. *Jer* 9. 3. *Ezek.* 22. 25. 2 *Tim.* 4. 10. *Hag.* 1. 2. *Phil.* 2. 21. *Rev.* 3. 15. 16. But alas! It is long ſince our Fathers had reaſon to complain and confeſs, that many in their day by perſwaſion or terror ſuffered themſelves to be divided and withdrawn to make defection to the contrary part : Many had turned

off to a deteftable indefferency and Neutrality in this Cau'e which fo much concerneth the Glory of God , and the good of thefe Kingdoms; Nay many had made it their ftudy to walk fo as they might comply with all times, and all the revolutions thereof. It was not their care to counte-nance, encourage, intruft, and employ fuch only, as from their hearts did affect and mind Gods work: But the hearts of fuch many times had been difcouraged, and their hands weakned, their fufferings neglected, and themfelves flighted ; And many who had been once open Enemies, and alwayes fecret Underminers, countenanced and employed; Nay, even thofe who had been looked upon as Incendiaries, and upon whom the Lord had fet Marks of defperate Malignancy, Falfhood and Deceit, were brought in as fit to manage publick Affairs. All which Sins and Breach-es of Covenant have now encreafed to a greater height of heinoufnefs ; For in our day, thefe Incendiaries, defperate and ingrained Malignants , have only been imployed in , and ad-mitted to the management of Affairs in Church and State, and none but they have been ac-counted *Habile* by Law : And fuch divifions from this Covenanted Conjunction, and defecti-ons to the contrary part, have been enacted and eftablifhed by Law. Yea, all the unhappy divifions that have been in our day, have been the woeful confequents and effects of Defecti-ons to the contrary part. At the firft erection of Prelacy , many, both Minifters and Profef-fors, partly by Terror and partly by Perfwafion. did withdraw from this Covenanted Con-junction, and make defection unto Prelacy, with which they combin'd in conforming with it, and fubmitting unto the Miniftry of the conforming Curats : And afterwards, by the terror of the fear of Men, and the perfwafions of their Counfels and Example, many of us have been feduced into a Combination with Malignants, in taking Oaths and Bonds contrary to the Co-venants, thereby dividing our felves from the Recufants, and making defection to the party impofing them, and oppofing the Covenants. And by Combination of thofe that preferred Peace to Truth, and Eafe to Duty, by the terror of threatned continuance of Perfecution, and the perfwafion of a promifed Relaxation and immunity from Troubles, many Minifters have been divided from the Teftimony of the Church of *Scotland* againft the encroach-ing Supremacy and Abfolute Power, and one from another, and have made defection to that part and Party that were advancing thefe Encroachments and Ufurpations on the prerogatives of Chrift and Priviledges of his Church, by receiving *Indulgences* and *Tolerations* from them; in their own nature deftructive unto, and given, and received on terms incon-fiftent with the Duties of the Covenants, which were contrived and conferred on purpofe to divide them from this caufe, and from their Brethren that more tenacioufly adhered to it, and did effectuate that defign in a great meafure. And others gave themfelves to a dete-ftable indifferency, in complying with, conniving at, and not witneffing againft thefe de-fections, but paffing them over in a fecure and fubmiffive filence : And yet many of us have not fhewed our diflike of thefe backfliding courfes, by difcountenancing, withdraw-ing from, and keeping our felves free of all participation with them : And others have with-drawn , that have not mourned for the fin of thefe things , to the irritation and offence, rather than conviction of thefe they withdrew from. Moreover, in the fame *Article* we are fworn, *all the dayes of our lives, zealoufly and conftantly to continue in this Caufe, againft all Letts and Impediments whatfoever : And, what we are not able our felves to fupprefs and overcome, to reveal and make known, that it may be timely prevented or removed.* And in the National Co-venant, " never to caft in any Lett or Impediment that may ftay or hinder any fuch refolution

"tlon as by common confent fhall be found to conduce for fo good ends; but on the con-
"trary, by all fawful means to labour to further and promove the fame. And if any fuch dan-
"gerous and d vifive motion be made to us by word or writ , that we and every one of us
"fh.ll either fuppreſs it, or if need be, incontinent make the fame known, that it may be time-
"oufly obviated; agreeing very well with Scriptures, *Num*: 14:9, 10: *Neh*: 6:3,6,8,9,10,11,&c.
Pfal: 69:9:*Ifa*: 8:12, 14: *Acts* 4: 19: *Acts* 20:24: & 21: 13: *Gal*: 2: 5: *Phil*: 1: 28, Neverthelefs,
many have been the lets and impediments that have been caſt in the way
to retard and obſtruct the Lords work, by Prelacy, Supremacy, Indulgences.
Tolleration, and abfolute Tyrannie, and compſyances therewith, enacted by Law; and
all the mifchiefs eſtabl fhed by a Throne of iniquity thefe 28. years. Yet few have ever zealoufly contented, and fewer have conſtantly continued in contending againſt thefe obſtructi-
ons, fo deſtructive to the caufe. Many have keeped Secret the firſt motions and appearances of thefe things, while they might have been fuppreſſed and overcome : And the
generality have paſſed them over in filence, and made not known, nor adverted unto the
Evil of thefe things when declared, by witneſſing againſt thefe things, when they could not
be otherwife removed or overcome. Yet many of us have our felves caſt in Lets and Impediments obſtructive to the Caufe, by our Defections, Divifions, and Diforders, againſt Common Confent, & precipitencies without cōmon confent, even of our Brethren adhering to the
Teſtimony. Many a divifive Motion hath not been counted dangerous, as thofe which tended
to divide us from the Covenanted Caufe; And many a good and neceſſary Motion, hath been
ccunted Divifive, namely fuch as propofed the neceſſity of confeſſing and forfaking fin.

Befides thefe, and many other breaches of the Articles of the Covenant, in the matter thereof, which concerneth everyone of us to fearch,
out and acknowledge before the Lord, as we would wifh his wrath to be
turned away from us; So have many of us failed exceedingly, in the
manner of following and purfuing the duties contained therein; not only
feeking great things for our felves, and mixing private interefts and
ends concerning our felves, and friends, and followers, with thefe things
that concern the publick good; but many times preferring fuch to the
honour of God, and good of his Caufe, and retarding Gods work, untill we might carry alongſt with us our own Interefts and Defigns. It
hath been our way to truſt in the means, and to rely upon the arm of
flefh for fuccefs, albeit the Lord many times hath made us meet with
difappointment therein, and ſtained the pride of all our glory, by bla-
ſting every carnal confidence unto us: We have followed, for the moſt
part, the counfels of flefh and blood, and walked more by the Rules of
Policy than Piety, and have hearkned more unto men than unto God.

In the *concluſion* of the Solemn League and Covenant, there is a Profeſſion and Declaration before GOD and the World of our unfeigned defires to be humbled *a* for
our own fins, and *b* for the fins of thefe Kingdoms, efpe-

a Ezk: 7: 16:
b Ezk: 9: 4:
c Matth: 22: 5:

cially that we have not *c* valued as we ought the ineſtimable benefite of the Gofpel, that we have not laboured

for

Power thereof, and that we have
receive Chrift in our hearts, nor to
m in our lives, h *which are the caufes*
reffions fo much abounding among us.
ny obligations to confefs and mourn over
f our true and unfeigned purpofe
ur for our felves, and all others under our power
ublick and in private, in all Duties we owe to God
ur Lives, and each one to go before another in the
formation, that the Lord might turn away His
fignation, and eftablifh thefe Churches and King-
eace; Yet we have refufed to be Reformed, and
and obftinatly againft the Lord, not valuing His
g our felves unto the obedience thereof, not feek-
ftudying to honour Him in the excellency of His
Him in the vertue of His Offices, not making
Ordinances, nor Private nor Secret Duties, nor
another in Love. The Ignorance of God, and of
revails exceedingly in the Land. Even our Fathers,
d in their Acknowledgement of Sins, That the greateft part
s among Noblemen, Barons, Gentlemen, Bur-
, neglected to feek God in their Families, and to
nation thereof. And albeit it had been much
the Nobles and Great Ones, —— could be
Family Duties themfelves in their own Perfons,
ry and ufeful a duty to be mifregarded by others

And we may add in our degenerate times, not only the
fe the neglect and contempt of fo neceffary and ufeful a duty,
and in the ufe of Chaplains, except fuch who are as Prophane as
l part of the Commons are altogether Strangers to it, many per-
orfhip; Others, only finging a Pfalm and Reading a Chapter,
rs, making a fafhion of performing all, but very perfunctori-
ently, and fcarce once in a day; And making litle Confcience in
their Children and Servants. The Nobility, Gentry
ould be examples of Godlinefs and Sober walking
ry generally Ring-leaders of excefs and Rioting.
: to reckon up all the Abominations that are in the
eming of the Name of God, fwearing by the
n of the Lords day, Uncleannefs, Drunkennefs,
Vanity of Apparrel, Lying and Deceit, Railing
I   and

d Acts 2: 42.
1 Tit: 6:13,14.
e 2 Tim: 3: 5:
f Ephef: 3: 17:
  Coloff: 2: 6:
g Coloff: 1: 10:
h 2 Thef: 2:.11,12:

and Curſing, Arbitrary and uncontrolled Oppreſſi
the faces of the Poor, by Landlords and others in [
become ordinary and common Sins. We have been
Lives, and promoting a perſonal Reformation, and going before o[
of a real Reformation, when we have been bad examples of Deform
ctiſes and publick Tranſactions, and being too familiar, and too [
and Patterns of all the Lands Deformations. Our Fathers alſo a
they were the Lords People, engaged unto Him into a S
had not made it their ſtudy that Judicatories and A
of, and places of Power and Truſt be filled with M
Chriſtian Converſation, and of known Integrity, a
affection and zeal unto the cauſe of God, And not
neutral and indifferent, but diſaffected and, Maligh
were profane and ſcandalous were intruſted: By wl
that Judicatories, even then, were the ſeats of Injuſtic
many in their Armies, by their miſcarriages, becau
the great prejudice of the Cauſe of God, the great [
and the great increaſe of looſeneſs and profanity thro
But we, their far more degenerate Children, have ſeen and ow
of, and filled with perjured Traitors to God and their Countrey
theſe Plagues, Marſhalled under a diſplayed Banner againſt the (
the Scandal, but for the Suppreſſion of the Goſpel, and forcing p
out the Land: Yet we have not ſighed nor cryed for theſe Abomi
concerned as we ought, with the abounding of them through the l
which in any meaſure we profeſſed intended it ſelf far beyond all
not regarding the Ignorance and Profanity of the many dark plac
Borders, Highlands, and Northern Iſles, and other parts; nor bein
knowledge of God and Religion among them. As likewiſe with
our Pride and preſumptuous boaſting of the External Priviledges v
of the Goſpel, and outward Reformation, and Teſtimony, which we
made us better than others: while we made not Conſcience of in
nor of bringing forth ſuitable Fruits in a perſonal Reforma
the conceitedneſs of ſome in Suffering, and Non-Complya:
Truth, rather for keeping up the Contention, and abetting a
under too lofty names of, the Suffering Party and Remnant
keep and hold faſt the Word of the Lords Patience, to His Glory
other evidences of pride, hateful to God, in boaſting of the uſe
way, and being too much taken up with them. (the neceſſary t
in a revengeful reſenting of affronts, in a paſſionate and diſdainf
For exceſſes in the manner of any duty, When we thought the ma
lightneſs of Carriage, forgetting our Sufferings ſince they began to
of our greateſt Sufferings, and ſince we got this Liberty of late,
regrate, that Idleneſs of both kinds, hath too much abounded
we were in a manner driven from the World, and ſhut up from
exerciſe of Godlineſs, many did not improve that opportunity o
acquaintance and communion with God, being ſlothful in Prayer, [

And some again, even since they might have had access to go to Service; or other lawful Employments, have continued idle and out of work , to the opening of the mouths of many against the Cause, albeit they were not called to, or employed in any publick businefs for the same. And besides all these things , there be many other transgressions , whereof the Land wherein we live are guilty, which we have not been humbled for to this day : But in stead of mourning for them, confessing and forsaking them , we have been rather defending or daubing, covering or colouring, excusing or extenuating them. All which we now defire to acknowledge, and be humble for, that the World may bear witnefs with us, that Righteousnefs belongeth unto God, and shame and confusion of face unto us, as appears this day.

BUT, because it is needful for these who find Mercy, not only to confefs, but also to forsake their sin; Therefore, that the reality and sincerity of our Repentance may appear, WE do Refolve, and Solemnly Engage our felves, before the Lord, carefully to avoid, for the time to come, all these Offences whereof we have now made folemn publick acknowledgement, and all the snares and tentations which tend thereunto: And to testifie the integrity of our Refolution herein , and that we may be the better enabled , in the power of the Lords strength to perform the fame; we do again Renew our Solemn League and Covenant, promising hereafter to make Conscience of all the Duties whereunto we are obliged in all the Heads and Articles thereof , particularly of these which follow.

Because Religion is of all things the moft excellent and precious, and the knowledge of the Great Truths of the Gofpel, fo generally decreased in this Land, is fo absolutely neceffary. Therefore, we shall endeavour to be better acquainted with the written Word of God, the only infallible Rule of Faith and Manners; And shall study, more than formerly, the Doctrine of this True Reformed Church, fummarly contained in our Confeffion of Faith, Catechifms larger and shorter, Sum of Chriftian Doctrine, and practical ufe of Saving Knowledge, Directory for publick Worship, Propofitions concerning Church Government and Ordination of Minifters, &c. And other Writings, clearing and confirming thefe Truths approven by this Church, and agreeable with the Word of God. The advancing and promoving the power of this True Reformed Religion, in our felves and others, against all Ungodlinefs and Profanity, And the fecuring and preferving the purity thereof against all Error, Herefie and Schifme, and namely Independency, Anabaptifme, Antinomianifme, Arminianifme, Socinianifme, Familifme, Libertinifme, Scapticifme, Quakerifme, and Eraftianifme, shall be more studied and endeavoured by us. And as we declare we willingly agree in our Confciences with this Doctrine of the Church of Scotland, in all points, as unto Gods undoubted Truth and Verity, grounded only upon His written Word; So, we refolve constantly to adhere unto, and maintain, and defend, and profefs, and confefs, and, when called of God, to be willing to suffer for every point of the said Doctrine, as we shal desire to be approven and confessed by Christ Jesus before God and His Holy Angels. 2. We shall also study more sincerity, uprightness, and heart integrity in the *Worship* of God, and not satisfy our selves with the forme of it, without the Spirituality that the Object of it requires; And shal endeavour to Recover and Preserve the Liberty and Purity thereof from all Corruptions, Novations, or Inventions of Men, Popish, Prelatical, Erastian, or any other. And if we cannot get these Corruptions Reformed and removed, we shal study to keep out selves free of Communion and Participation with the same. 3. We shall likewise, by all Lawful means, endeavour the Recovery and Re-establishment of *Presbyterial Government*, which is the only order of Christs House of Divine Institution, and seek to have it Redintegrated in all its parts, Priviledges, and Courts of Kirk *Sessions*, *Presbytries*, *Synods*, and *General Assemblies*. And that the true *Discipline* of the same Church may be impartially Exercised; Both which, we shall endeavour to Preserve aginst all that seek to Subvert and Pervert the same: And when Restored and Recovered in its freedom and integrity; shall Cordially submit unto the same, as becomes the Flock of Christ. 4. In like manner, the carrying on the Work of Uniformity. in the three Kingdoms, shall be desired, designed, prayed for, studied and endeavoured by us, by Remonstrances, Supplications, Admonitions, Testimonies, and all other means possible; lawful, expedient and competent unto us in our capacities, and that before all Worldly Interests whether concerning the Magistrate, or our selves, or any other whatsomever.

According to the *Second Article*, 1. We shall do our outmost endeavours to have the Land purged of *Popish Idolatry*, the Monuments thereof destroyed, and so far as lies in our power, shall never suffer the same to be reintroduced or erected again : But shall endeavour to have the *Penal Statutes* against Papists, of late stopped and suspended by the Tolleration, revived, left in full force, and duely put in execution against those Enemies of Religion and all good Government. 2. We shal Endeavour the extirpation of *Prelacy*, by all approven means, according to our Capacities and Vocations, And in order thereto, we shall never submit to that Prelatical Hierarchy of *Arch-bishops*, *Bishops*, &c. having power of Order or Jurisdiction over preaching *Presbyters* , whether Erastian, or only Diocesan, in any form or degree, howsoever Reformed, accommodated, restricted, or limited by Cautions or provisions of Men; Since frequent and fatal experience hath taught this Church , that they cannot be kept long within banks or bounds; And the Word of God hath condemned that Office, and *Subordination* it self, in any degree. We shall also, by all lawful and legal means, seek the removing of their substitute *Curats*, depending on them; from the Parish-Churches on which they have intruded. And shall never submit to the Ministry of, hear, or receive Ordinances from, nor pay any Stipends unto any Man that enters into the Cure of any Parish. at the door of the Bishops Collation, or Patrons Presentation. 3. Because many have of late laboured to supplant the Liberties of the Kirk, and have in a great measure obtained their design, by the late *Indulgences* and *Toleration*, We shall refuse, withstand, and witness against all such Encroachments on the Liberties of this Church in all times coming ; And shal withdraw our selves from Communion with any such Meetings or Congregations, that hold their freedom from, and are modified by such Usurpations. Purposing and promising to use all endeavours to have a settled Ministry, according to Christs Institution, without any dependence on, subordination unto, or homologation of an Ecclesiastick Erastian & usurped supremacy in the Civil Magistrate. Furthermore, we shal strive to recover, & when recovered, Maintain and Defend the Kirk of *Scotland*, in all her Liberties and Priviledges according to our power, against all who shall oppose or undermine the fame, or encroach thereupon, under any pretext whatfomever. 4. And as on the one hand, we here enter into Vowes to deteft and abhor all Superftition, Herefie, and Profanenefs, and whatfoever fhall be found contrary to found Doctrine and the power of Godlinefs, and to keep our felves, fo far as we can, from all partaking in other Mens fins, by confent unto, affociation, incorporation, combiration, communion, complyance with, or conniving at their fins; So, We refolve, in the Lords ftrength, to guard againft all Schifme and finful Separation, or unjuft, rafh, and diforderly withdrawing from Congregations, Societies, or Families, or any part of the Communion of the true Reformed Covenanted Church of *Scotland*, holding purely and intirely the Doctrine, Worfhip, Difcipline and Government of the fame in Principle and Exercife, according to the Rules of Chrift, and ftanding Acts and Conftitutions of this Church. And that we fhall neither gather nor fet up formed feparate Churches or Societies, under other Ordinances, Government or Miniftry, diftinct from the Presbyterian Church of *Scotland*. Nor withdraw from Minifter or Member of that Body, for any offence, in any cafe, where either the offence may be legally removed without our withdrawing; Or cannot be inftructed to be condemned by the Word of God, or the Conftitutions of this Church; Or is in it felf an infufficient ground of withdrawing; Or a thing to be condefcended upon, forborn, or forgiven. But fhall ftudy to maintain Union and Communion, in Truth and Duty with all the Minifters and Members of the faid Church, that do, and in fo far as they do follow the Inftitutions of Chrift.

According to the *Third Article*, 1. We fhall endeavour with all fincerity, reality and conftancy, according to our Vocations and Capacities, by all poffible & lawful means, to feek the removal of thofe things that corrupt, prelimite, or preclude the right conftitution of Parliaments, and other Judicatories; The refcinding and taking away of thefe wicked Acts and Oaths that give entrance unto the Enemies of the Reformation, to fit there as Members, and exclude thofe that are honeft and well affected to the Covenant and Caufe of God. And all other Acts and Laws that have been framed fince Prelacy and Tyranny came in, that have been oppofite unto the faid Covenant and work of Reformation; The reviving and ratifying of all former Righteous Laws, made in favours thereof; And the reftoring and recovering of all the due and true Rights and Priviledges of Parliaments. And as we fhall earneftly pray unto God that He would give us *able men fearing God, men of Truth, and hating covetoufnefs*, to judge and bear Charge among His people; So, we fhall according to our Places, Callings and Capacities endeavor that Judicatories and all places of Power and Truft, both in Kirk and State, may confift of, and be filled with fuch men as are of known good Affection to the Caufe of *God*, and of a blamelefs and Chriftian converfation, to whom we fhall fubmit, and obey, and defend them and their Rights, with our Eftates and Lives. 2. We fhall alfo defire, and do defign to recover, vindicate and maintain the Liberties of the Subjects, in all thefe things which concern their Confciences, Perfons and Eftates, 3. Now after we have been long howling under a grievous Tyrannie, making men like the fifhes of the Sea that have no Ruler over them; We fhall defire and long for a good Government, and feek to have it rightly fetled, upon fuch a foundation of Righteoufnefs, with fuch a fubordination to God, and in fuch hands as Religion and Liberty, and we in maintaining the fame, may find protection and Patrociny. And then in the terms of the Covenant, we promife Subjection, Allegiance, and our beft endeavours to preferve and defend the Perfon and Authority of our Lawfully invefted Kings, Princes, or other Magiftrates, in the prefervation and defence of the True Religion, and Liberties of the Kingdom, Miniftration

niftration of Juftice, and punifhing of iniquity : Or fo far as our owning and defending them may, or can confift with the prefervation and defence of Religion, Liberty and Juftice ; Giving unto GOD that which is GODS , and to Cæfar the things which are Cæfars : And upon other termes, we purpofe never to own Allegiance to mortall Man.

According to the Fourth Article , 1. Being now fenfible of the fin of complyance with Malignants, we fhall refolve through Grace to ftand aloof, and at a greater diftance from every thing that may import complyance, confederacy, or [unitive tranfaction with them while remaining fuch, by Affociating with them in Armes, paying them Ceffes and Contributions impofed for maintaining them in their Caufe and courfe of oppofition to the Caufe of GOD; Or by fwearing, fubfcribing, or taking any of their Oaths, Tefts or Bonds; Or any new Oaths or Bonds whatfoever , which may any way condemn, Limite, or Reftrain us in the Duties whereunto we are obliged by the National or Solemn League and Covenant. Yea, 2. We fhall be fo far from conniving at, complying with , or countenancing of Malignancy, Injuftice, Iniquity, Profanity and Impiety , that we fhall not only avoid and difcountenance thefe things , and cherifh and encourage thefe perfons who are zealous for the Caufe of GOD, and walk according to the Gofpel : But alfo fhall feek a more effectual courfe than heretofore , in our refpective places and Callings , for punifhing and fuppreffing thefe evils , and faithfully endeavour that the beft and fitteft remedies may be applyed for taking away the caufes thereof, and advancing the knowledge of GOD, and Holinefs and Righteoufnefs in the Land. And to this effect, fhall endeavour to Reprefent our Grievances unto competent Judicatories againft thofe who have been open Perfecuters , that they may receive condign punifhment as the degree of their Crimes and Offences fhall require or deferve, that fo the Land may be purged from blood , and the LORD may delight to dwell among us. Ye confidering what rafhnefs hath appeared in fome, in putting forth their hand to punifh fuch Incendiaries by death , and how people may be ftill in hazard of running upon Extravagances in this matter, from the mifunderftanding of this Article of the Covenant ; We fhal therefore guard againft all irregularities in feeking the punifhment of Malignants, Incendiaries, or evil Inftruments, and endeavour the difcoverie and bringing of them to Juftice in a Right and Legal way.

According to the Fifth Article, We fhal according to our places, power, & Intereft, endeavour to have the Union of the Kingdoms brought to its Covenanted Bafis, and avoid every thing that may weaken the fame , or involve us in any meafure of acceffion unto the guilt of thofe who have invaded, or hereafter may invade the Kingdom of England to break this Covenanted Union. And fhall endeavour more correfpondence and fympathie with all our Covenanted Brethren, both in England and Ireland.

According to the Sixth Article , Confidering what Dangers , We, and all our Brethren, under the Bond , and owning the Obligation of thefe Covenants , are in, and may be expofed to, from the Popifh Prelatical and Malignant Faction ftill prevailing, And what defects we are fenfible have been among us in the duty of defending and affifting one another in this caufe. We do here folemnly enter under a Bond of Affociation with all that do now renew thefe Covenants with the Acknowledgement of the publick Breaches, and Engagement to the duties, thereof, and fhall concert and affert the old Covenanted Caufe and Quarsel, as our Fathers stated and contended for it, from the year 1638. to 1650. Which cause of the Covenanted Reformation, in Doctrine, Worship, Discipline and Government, and all Interests and Rights Religious or Civil, contended for, during that foresaid space of years conducing to promote the same; we faithfully promise to prosecute, and endeavour to propagate, preserve and maintain, with the hazard of our Lives and all that we have. Not fearing or regarding the foul Aspersions of *Rebellion, Combination*, or what else our Adversaries from their Craft and Malice would put upon us. Seing what we do is so well warranted, and ariseth from an unfeigned desire to maintain the true Religion, to obtain the Protection, and preserve the Honour of Righteous Government, and promote the Peace and Happiness of the Kingdom, for the present Safety and future Felicity of our Selves and Posterity, and encouragement of others, groaning under, or in danger of the Yoke of *Antichristian* or *Eraslin, Popish* or *Prelatical Tyranny*, to joyn in the same or like *Association*. In maintaing which, we shall faithfully and stedfastly, according to our place and power, sympathize, beat all burdens, and imbark our Interests with, and assist and defend all these who enter into or joyn with this *Association* and *Covenants*. And shall reckon whatsoever shal be done to the least of us for this Cause, as done to us all in general, and to every one of us in particular. And shal account it a breach of Covenant, if, seing our Brethren pursued for this Cause, and having sufficient means to comfort and assist them, any of us shall either make peace with the Persecuters, bind up their hands by Oaths or Bonds from resisting them, refuse to bide, harbour or supply the Persecuted, decline to venture in lawful and necessary attempts for their relief, or withdraw from their dutiful support. And being thus united and Associate in this Cause, as we resolve and oblige our selves to abide in this firm conjunction, and neither consent nor concede to any Combination or Counsel, suggestion, perswasion, allurement or terror that may have any direct or indirect tendency, tentation or influence to seduce us, either to division among our selves, or defection to our Adversaries, or a base indifferency & neutrality between the two, but shall with all Zeal, Fidelity and constancy communicate our best help, counsel and concurrence for the promoving all resolutions, as by common consent shall be found to conduce for the good of the cause. And endeavour to discover, oppose and suppress all contrivances or counsels that may cast in any let or impediment that may be obstructive or prejudicial to the cause: So we shall likewise desire, design and endeavour to get the defections, unworthy neutralities, and unhappy divisions that have long and lamentably wounded and wracked this Church, removed; Differences settled, and Breaches healed, in such a way, and upon such terms as may be honourable and advantagious for the *Cause*. And if our Brethren and we, between whom such differences have fallen in and have been sadly fomented on all hands, will search and try our wayes respectively, how far they and we have receded from the *good Old Way* of the *Church* of *Scotland*, and in our impartial search, shall find out our respective defections and breaches of Covenant, on the one hand and on the other, and unite in confessing these, by joyning in this or the like acknowledgement of publick sins, and keeping days of Humiliation and Mourning for the same. And as we offer and promise to confess our sins here acknowledged, or any other (so far as we can be convinced) any manner of way that they shall desire or appoint; So, if they will at least confess theirs Doctrinally, and they and we both forsake them mutually; And forsaking, concur in procuring the condemnation of them in Ecclesiastical synods or Assemblies, and so return unto, and fix our ground on the Old established Foundations, according to the Word of God and Constitutions of this Church, settled before the Covenanted Reformation stopped: We will then embrace and maintain Union and Communion with them, and offer and avouch our concurrence with them, and submission to them in the Lord: And shall not suffer our selves, directly or indirectly, by whatsoever combination, perswasion or terror, to be divided and withdrawn from this blessed Union and Conjunction.

And

And becaufe there be many, who heretofore have not made Confcience of the Oath of God, but fome through fear, others by perfwafion, and upon bafe ends and humane Interefts have entered thereunto, who have afterwards difcovered themfelves to have dealt deceitfully with the Lord, in fwearing falfly by His Name. Therefore We who do now re-new our Covenants in reference to thefe duties, and all other duties con-tained therein, Do, in the fight of Him who is the fearcher of hearts, Solemnly Profefs, that it is not upon any Politick advantage, or Pri-vate Intereft, or by-end or becaufe of any terror or perfwafion from men, or hypocritically or deceitfully, that we do again take upon us the *oath of God*, But honeftly and fincerely, and from the fenfe of our Duty: And that therefore denying our felves and our own things, and laying afide all felf-interefts and ends, we fhall above all things feek the Ho-niour of GOD, the good of His Caufe, and the wealth of His People; And that forfaking the counfels of flefh and blood, and not leaning upon Carnal confidence, we fhall depend upon the LORD, walk by the Rule of His Word, and hearken to the voice of His Servants. In all which, profeffing out own weaknefs, we do earneftly pray to GOD, who is the Father of Mercies, through His Son *Jefus Chrift*, to be mer-ciful unto us, and to enable us by the power of His Might, that we may do our Duty, unto the praife of His Grace in the Churches. *AMEN.*

F I N I S

.

www.ingramcontent.com/pod-product-compliance
Lightning Source LLC
Chambersburg PA
CBHW021529270326
41930CB00008B/1160